Angel Warrior

Sharon Luca

Angel Warrior
Authored by Sharon Luca

The author has recreated events, locales and conversations from her memories of them. In order to maintain anonymity, in most instances the author has changed the names of individuals and places, and may have changed some identifying characteristics and details, such as physical properties, occupations and places of residence.

DEDICATION

To the memory of my son, Luca, whom I love and miss with all my heart, each and every day.

To Almighty God, helping me in my darkest days to find my faith again, and for giving me the strength to carry on as the clouds of sorrow and despair have begun to lift.

To my son, Ky, and my husband, Jas, who have kept me going. Since losing Luca, followed by the chronic pain of fibromyalgia, Ky has literally helped me to get out of bed each morning. My husband has also been by my side every step of the way, for which I will always be grateful.

Finally, my close family and friends who have been there to support me when I've needed them. I will be forever grateful for your kindness.

ACKNOWLEDGMENTS

I have so many people to thank for helping me put this book together, and I will start with my wonderful husband, Jas. He has been my rock throughout the whole of the traumatic experience of losing Luca, despite the fact that he was in deep grief himself. He encouraged me to put my feelings down on paper, not only as a healing tool for myself, but also as a kind of road map for families who have had the misfortune to lose a still-born child. I am eternally grateful to him for that.

In addition, I would like to thank Shelley Wilson, Writing Solutions, for guiding me on the road to writing this book. I would also like to thank Marie Rowe, who has had extensive book and script editing experience in the Hollywood film industry. She kindly stepped in to edit my book, and has done this with great care and sensitivity, for which I am very grateful. I am also grateful to Karen Heap of Orchard Developments for her invaluable business advice regarding setting up my clothing line: LK Eco Style. Karen is always patient and kind, and nothing is too much trouble for her. Likewise, Sandra Garlick of Woman Who has been a wonderful inspiration in all my ventures. She has been, and continues to be, a great source of encouragement, which I so appreciate. The wonderful Andrea Rainsford has helped me get online visibility for LK Eco Style, and Emma Green of "Luna Creative Design" has done an amazing job designing my website, as well as my clothing line. Amanda Chalmers from 'Chalmers PR', is another incredible lady who has been involved in promoting me, the charity and my business. With her nomination I was chosen as '1 in 30 Amazing Women in the UK' for "Take a Break" magazine, which was a huge thrill.

To all my close family and friends who have supported me on this hard journey so far. You know who you are! Thank you for your understanding when I cancel plans late in the day due to fatigue & pain. Also, for your continued support and love on Luca's birthday each year. It means so much to Jas and I knowing you have not forgotten our first son.

And finally, and most important, the Lord himself, who has made my faith stronger. Coventry Cathedral has become my place of inner peace and played a huge part in this journey to date. It is the place where my prayers are answered and where ideas have come to me.

DONATIONS & SUPPORT

10% of the profits from this book will support the work of The Luca Foundation

www.thelucafoundation.org.uk

You can also purchase my book: 'Why Did Grandad Die?' on this website. This book supports the mental health of children when explaining bereavement, and all profits go to The Luca Foundation.

In addition, you can purchase your 'Angel Warrior' tee-shirt from LK Eco Style

www.lkecostyle.com

Using code AW25, bereaved parents will receive 25% off their purchase of the 'Angel Warrior' range of clothing & accessories.

Follow The Luca Foundation at:
Instagram: @thelucafoundation
Twitter: @foundationluca
Facebook page: The Luca Foundation
Follow LK Eco Style at:
Instagram: @lk_eco_style
Twitter: @eco_lk
Facebook page: LK Eco Style

Soon to come: LK Media. This is where we will invite more parents to blog and open up about their child loss journey and help others through theirs. If this is something you would like to be part of, please email me at: info@lkecostyle.com.

CONTENTS

Introduction

Before I met Jas, my future husband, there was a lot of planning behind the scenes to get us together. My cousin and another distant family member who played football with Jas, thought we would make the perfect couple. So, they spoke to us both and we agreed to exchange email addresses.

The first time Jas emailed me I could sense the nervousness in his wording. It was quite cute. We did a little bit of general chit-chat, just to get to know the basics of each other really. Then I thought: well, I'm going to lay everything on the line, be upfront and honest because I didn't want to waste his time.

Jas is Indian and from a Sikh family but atheist himself, so I explained that I was not your average Indian; I'm Christian by faith and my family are a mix of cultures. I told him that I had been married, but was a victim of domestic abuse, so was now divorced. I said if any of this was a problem for him, he should tell me right away. He thanked me for being honest and told me he thought honesty and trust were key in starting any relationship. He assured me that what I'd told him about my past wasn't a problem for him and that we all had history. He also explained that he hadn't been married, but had been in a committed relationship, which came to an end a couple of years before. I asked if he thought his family would have an issue with anything I had told him. He was adamant that, if down the line, we chose to be together, it didn't matter what the family said; it was about what made us happy. This was quite a relief to me, as my ex-husband had been quite the opposite – wanting approval from family members, and doing anything to get it, rather than making sure I was happy. Of course, I hadn't known this until I'd entered into the marriage, which had been arranged quickly. Thankfully, there's never been an arranged marriage in my family since. In fact, we've all been free to marry whomever we wanted. The family definitely learnt a lot from that disastrous marriage.

After a couple of weeks of emailing, Jas suggested we meet, and I only agreed to this because I was close to my cousin and didn't want to disappoint her. But I wasn't really expecting much to come of this. I'd been on other blind dates, which were awful, so I always made sure I had a backup call planned: where a friend would call me half an hour into my meeting with the blind date, just in case I didn't like the guy and then I'd have an excuse for a quick getaway.

We decided to meet on a Saturday for drinks. Unfortunately, I had to rearrange because I came down with an awful cold. I was in bed for three days and off work. Although Jas decided to play golf with his friends, he did text me a few times over that weekend to find out how I was feeling. I thought how sweet and caring he was and felt quite comforted by that.

When eventually we did meet at a bar, there was certainly a physical attraction, because Jas is so good looking. But the main thing was, we were really comfortable talking to one another. It was as if we'd known each other a while, but of course we had been talking by email and text quite a lot, which had broken the ice. We talked about football – he's an Everton supporter and I'm an Arsenal fan. It was during the 2008 Euros, so we discussed the teams who were favoured to win the competition. A couple of hours went by so quickly and we departed on a good note, neither of us actually saying that we would meet up again. I suppose for me I just wanted to hear it from him; but because Jas is quite shy, he prefers to do things by text.

Well, he did text and we arranged to meet again. I didn’t know, however, that the night we had arranged to meet was when Spain were playing in the Euros, so I actually rearranged our date by text. In his reply, he asked me if everything was okay and I said: “Yes, but I just didn't realise when we set the date that Spain were playing that night, and I want to watch the match.” He sent me a message saying: “L.O.L! I can’t believe I’ve actually met a woman who would cancel a date for a football match! It’s flipping fantastic!”

During the first few weeks I was dating Jas, an aunt of mine had called my mother saying that at her son's wedding, which was coming up, she’d like to introduce me to her husband's nephew. At this point my mum didn't know that I was seeing Jas. I hadn’t told her, as I was still getting to know him, but the idea of meeting somebody else just turned my stomach. I did really like Jas though, and we had a good connection. Nonetheless, I went along with it knowing that I wouldn't be interested. As soon as the 'potential mate' was pointed out to me at the wedding, I just said 'no' and left it at that.

After I'd been seeing Jas for a couple of months, and knowing that I really liked him, and the feeling was mutual, I decided I wanted him to meet my brothers. It had to be within a certain timeframe, because my brother, Sunny, was in the Armed Forces and was on leave, and Steven had come back from working in London to spend a week at home in the Midlands. Jas agreed and we all met at a bar. He was so quiet compared to the Jas I knew. The three guys did talk a little about football, as there was a match playing at the time on the TV in the background. When Jas went to the restroom, my brothers laughed and asked if he ever spoke. I explained that he was probably nervous around them and that he wasn't normally like that at all. Well, it turned out I was right. Jas told me later that he felt nervous and shy and didn't know what to say. Now, after we've been together for twelve years, he's well and truly 'one of the lads' with my brothers.

A couple of weeks later we decided to take our first holiday together - a few days in Barcelona. It was fantastic and was a time to really open up and get to know each other even more. We went to the Camp Nou Stadium, which we both enjoyed even though I had been there before with my cousin, Karen. We had a great time looking around, eating, taking photos. We were both so interested in the same things. It was wonderful! I knew he was the one. We came back refreshed and got stuck back into work. I was a Business Development Manager in a corporate firm but wasn't having the greatest time at work. A lot of changes had taken place and I was a bit stressed about it.

A month after our holiday in Barcelona, Jas suggested we go away for a few days again, to get my mind off it all. I agreed I needed a break. At this time, my parents were away on holiday, so I suggested he come and stay with me so that he could get to know my German Shepherd, Kane. He was a big dog and was quite intimidating, but when Kane liked someone, he was soft. Kane was my baby and if Jas had not liked him, it would have been a deal-breaker. In my head, I had already imagined that if Jas and I got married, Kane would come to live with us. So I gently introduced him to Jas. I could see that he already adored Kane, and to my great relief, the feeling was mutual. We booked our holiday to Fuerteventura in the Canary Islands for early November. In our household we always took it in turns to take our holidays so that there was always someone at home for Kane. He officially belonged to my brothers and I, but my parents were just as attached to him, and they were always happy to take care of him.

It was beautifully warm on our holiday and it was nice to be away with Jas. We went to a bar on some days to watch the football, walked around and explored the area on other days, and then lay by the pool and just chilled. One evening, we were at a restaurant and had both had a couple of drinks. We were talking about his friend who was getting married, and because I was a bit tipsy, which made me bold, I asked Jas what he thought about marriage. He said that if he was with the right person, he would definitely get married. I asked, cheekily: “Have you met the right person yet?” He smiled and said: “I love you.” This was the first time he’d said those three little words. Then he said: “And ‘yes’ you’re the right person, Sharon.” I was overjoyed. “That's good, because I love you too, Jas!” Then we hugged and kissed. It was such a beautiful moment. "Now I guess we should tell our families," I said.

Jas was going to drop me off at home when we got back to England, so I suggested that perhaps he could meet my parents then. He was quite okay with that, so I texted my mum and told her what time we'd be back and that I'd like her and Dad to meet Jas. She was delighted that finally they were going to get to meet him. Mum had made dinner and chatted with Jas to find out about him and his family. Kane was walking around showing that he was extremely comfortable with Jas, but then came to have cuddles with me, as we always missed each other when I was away. My dad came home shortly after and also had a good conversation with Jas. After Jas had left, they both told me that they really liked him, and I was glad.

Now it was time for Jas to tell his family. He said he would talk to his mum first since she knew he was seeing somebody, although he'd never given her any details. She was surprised and pleased when he told her he wanted to marry me, but obviously wanted to know more. He told her a few things about me and then went to tell his dad. His dad was really happy and wanted to see a photo of me. So Jas texted me and asked me to send some photos for his dad to see. He added: LOL! I laughed and sent him photos. His dad said he was pleased with what he saw and asked when they would get to meet me. We arranged for us all to meet at his family home In Coventry. I was so nervous, I really didn't know what to expect, but luckily it went really well.

It was my cousin's twenty-first birthday party the following week and I knew my grandad would be there. I decided to tell him that I had met Jas and we wanted to get married. He was delighted and surprised because he always thought I would marry a British white man. He asked if I was sure I wanted to marry an Indian British guy. I laughed and told him that I did.

When I first started talking to Jas, I was really surprised to find out that we were both born on the same day – 16th March. What are the chances of that? Well, in March the following year we went to Egypt for a holiday to celebrate. The pyramids were amazing, of course, and the camels too. It was so different from anywhere else we'd visited. It was also hot, just the way I like it, and one day we decided to take a trip into the desert and mountains on quad bikes. It was so much fun. We stopped at the bottom of a hill-top and had a drink before going up the hill. We went quite high up and could see so much of the country and the desert. It was very peaceful. We took some photos and then Jas bent down on one knee and I thought he was going to do up his shoelace, but it was right there and then that he proposed to me. I was delighted. He didn't have a ring because he had no idea what kind of ring to get me, and thought it better that I choose one myself, which I was happy with. I was very glad to have had such a romantic and memorable proposal in a beautiful and exotic country.

Now we were officially engaged, we went to the Jewellery Quarter in Birmingham so that I could pick out an engagement ring. My fingers are quite small, so I had to have one made specially, which was great because I got to design it my-self. I chose a beautiful one-carat cushion-cut diamond, sitting on a crown of small diamonds with diamonds down the neck of the ring. It was perfect.

We had quite a small formal engagement party at

my parent's home. Jas's family came and met my family. It was then that my dad and Uncle remembered that they used to play football with Jas's uncles back in the 1970s. Small world, hey? They were all laughing and reminiscing about the olden days. My grandad was so happy. It wasn't very often that we saw him merry, but on this occasion, he was, and beaming with pride.

Whilst I was in Egypt, my dad had noticed that something wasn't quite right with Kane. When I came back, he said he thought Kane needed to go the vet as he'd got a lump on his throat. I felt around the dog's throat area and sure enough there was a small lump there. The vet detected something and said that she would need to keep Kane in for a day to do some tests. He didn't really like going to the vet, so it was a bit of a mission to leave him there. It was almost like settling a baby at nursery. I had to stay with him until he was comfortable.

I got a call in the afternoon and the vet confirmed that Kane had lymphoma. I was devastated when I took the call and knew that we wouldn't have him for long. My mum and I sobbed, and I suggested we got our tears out then before he came home. I didn't want Kane to see our tears. When I went to the vet to pick him up, he ran out with joy and jumped up at me to lick my face. I could tell he had missed me and was happy to see me, just as I was to see my beloved Kane. He was given steroid medication and something else to keep him going. The vet couldn't put a time limit on the length of his life but said if he took well to the medication, he could continue to have a good life. This was very reassuring, so we went home, and I made him some of his favourite food.

A couple of weeks after the engagement party, my parents had planned to go to Turkey on holiday. The day they were due to leave, Kane was in a bad way and could hardly move. My mum woke me up and told me and I rushed downstairs to Kane. I could see in his face that he was defeated, and I decided this was it. I called my brothers and asked them to come home and say their goodbyes to Kane, because the time had come for him to go. Sunny was down at the base and Steven was in London, so he was able to come home easily. But with Sunny being in the Armed Forces, we weren't sure whether he would be able to get back. He was relieved when his General said he understood the importance of the situation, as he was a dog owner himself, and he allowed Sunny to take leave.

My parents left for Turkey that afternoon, and because they knew Kane wouldn't be there on their return, they sobbed as they left the house. I cried as well as I said goodbye to them, knowing what was to come. My mum had called my aunt to come over to support me through this ordeal. My uncle and Aunt arrived about an hour before Sunny and Steven. I had called Jas in the afternoon to explain what was happening. He played football on Saturdays, so he hadn't heard my messages. When he did call back and I was crying, he said he'd come over immediately. Sunny's girlfriend, Olivia, was there too, as well as Steven's girlfriend, Grace. It was a chance for everyone to say their goodbyes to Kane.

I had called the vet that afternoon and asked her to come to the house; I didn't want Kane to suffer any longer.

I knew that if anyone was going to lift Kane's mood, it would be my brothers. He saw Sunny as his master, Steven his buddy who played games with him, and I was his carer. Sunny and Steven arrived quite soon after each other. Steven was first but there wasn't really a change in Kane's mood, although he had moved his position slightly when he saw Steven. When Sunny came in the door, Kane walked a few steps towards him and then lay down again. It was clear to us all that he had had enough. I had decided when the vet arrived that only Sunny, Steven and I would be with Kane for his last moments.

About an hour or so later, the vet arrived. My brothers and I sat on the floor next to Kane stroking him, kissing his nose, and acting as though everything was fine. The last thing we wanted was for Kane to feel nervous or anxious in his last moments. I was whispering to him: "Good boy…well done…good boy," while the vet administered the needle. My lovely dog was looking at me, and then suddenly, he was gone. The three of us rested our foreheads on Kane's lifeless body and cried our eyes out. It was the most horrible feeling - losing our beloved dog who'd been with our family for eight years.

Everyone came out from the lounge when they heard us crying, and my uncle took me in his arms. I snuggled on his shoulder and then Jas came in and he held me. I couldn't stop crying.

Grace was comforting Steven and Sunny was comforted by Olivia. After a short while the vet said we needed to take him to the car, and she gave us a blanket to put underneath him. As I said before, he was a large dog, around nine stone, so it took the strength of both Sunny and Steven to pick him up. Kane belonged to all three of us since we lived at home together when we first got him, so we all carried him out for this final time, sobbing our hearts out, knowing we'd never see him again.

When my parents came back from their holiday they walked in and cried as there was now no Kane to greet them. There was certainly a big void in the house without him. After a few weeks, my mum said she couldn't stand the emptiness and that she wanted to get another dog. I suggested we waited a little longer, although I had been feeling the same too. When Sunny came back on leave we discussed the idea and he said he was heartbroken too, but he didn't think another dog was going to help. Mum was adamant she wanted another dog. I was fifty-fifty. Mum saw an advert about pedigree German Shepherds for sale near Birmingham. Sunny agreed to go and have a look but commented that another dog was not going to be another Kane. Mum acknowledged that two dogs can't be the same, just as two people aren't alike.

So Mum, Sunny, Olivia and I went off to see the litter of puppies. Well, I bet you know what happened here. We all fell in love with a cute little German Shepherd puppy with a bit of red colouring. He seemed like the most well-behaved puppy out of the whole litter. We knew we wanted a male dog, and since he was the one we all felt most comfortable with, we put a deposit down for him there and then, and arranged to collect him three weeks later. My mum asked me to pick a name for him. Sunny and I laughed about the way the three of us (Sunny, Steven and I) had chosen Kane's name. You see we'd been big wrestling fans in the early 2000s, and I wanted to call the dog 'The Rock', as he was my favourite wrestler. We were going through the list of all the names of wrestlers we could think of, but none seemed right. Then, almost simultaneously, we all looked at each other and said "Kane!" and that was the one that stuck.

My mum's favourite film was 'Troy', or at least one of her favourites, and she loved that name. So, as this new German Shepherd was going to be hers and my dad's, although he was quite annoyed that we were getting another dog so soon, Mum picked the name Troy. I called Anne, the breeder, and asked her to start calling the dog, Troy, so that he got used it. She loved the name.

A few weeks later, Troy was with us in our big family home. He was certainly no Kane - he was a little devil, with more energy than he had shown on the day we went to see him. My goodness, he was hard work as a puppy but so cute at the same time. It was June 2009 by now.

The following month my grandad decided he wanted to go to India with his sons. My dad has three brothers and two of them were to go with him. They were all looking forward to it. I dropped my dad off at the airport in Birmingham and then went to see my grandad to wish him a good holiday and give him a big hug. There was something different about my grandad that day. He was overjoyed to be going, but also talking in a way that suggested he wasn't coming back. Then he used a phrase, something like: "If I come back." I said: "What do you mean, if?" and he laughed.

Whilst having a good time in the family village in India, one evening my grandad collapsed. He died quite quickly in my dad's arms. We were all devastated when we heard the news. I couldn't believe it. My grandad had gone. He was eighty-three. The funeral took place within the week, in India. Two of my aunts and cousins went over right away, because the cremation would be taking place within days of my grandad's death.

A few months later, at the end of October, I had planned to go to India with my mum, my grandma, and my cousin. We visited my grandad's estate, but it didn't feel the same without him there; it made me cry. Even though it was a sad time, we went to Punjab to do my wedding shopping. I had designed my own wedding outfit and wanted to have it made In India. I also wanted to purchase gifts of clothing for my new in-laws. I was delighted my mum's cousin was there as well. It was great fun staying at her house and taking her shopping with us. It was also lovely to see my mum's relatives who hadn't seen her for many years and to hear childhood stories about my mum. The shopping was a success, and we were back home after two weeks. Jas and I stayed in contact via our mobile phones. I couldn't wait to get back to see him; I missed him so much.

Jas and I had already started looking for a house before I had gone away, and he'd continued searching and had compiled a list of houses we could go and see. We soon found one that we really loved. It was a four-bedroomed detached home that was not too far from my family - sort of in the middle really, between both families. We put in an offer on the house, which was accepted, and we were excited about getting things moving.

By the New Year, we were in a good place - all the searches had been done, and we were getting ready to exchange contracts. This was a very exciting time for us. We planned to do so much to the house to make it our own and knew that we would be able to get started on renovations prior to the wedding. However, approximately ten days before we were due to sign the papers, the seller backed out. I was crushed. We'd been so excited as we knew this would be a lovely home for us, and we'd already ordered furniture. The seller had withdrawn because, apparently, he wasn't well, but we were still so upset and even had to pay the solicitor's fees for all the work he'd done.

We were now desperately trying to find a home. We started looking again and by March, three weeks before our wedding, we found a house that we really liked in Warwickshire. We put in an offer that evening and after a couple of calls, we negotiated a price that was agreed. We urged the solicitor to hurry things along. It was a vacant property so all we were waiting for were the searches, since our mortgage was already in place. Things developed quickly, and five days before our wedding, we signed and exchanged contracts. It had been quite a manic time, but we were relieved, nonetheless.

It was now April and our wedding was due to take place in a few days. Snow had been forecast, so we were panicking a little. I do like to be in control of things, but you can't control the weather. Overall, everything was fine, and I was on a high as I was going to marry my soulmate.

The wedding was on Easter Sunday, symbolic for me as a Christian starting a new life. On the Friday before - Good Friday - we had a henna party at my mum's house. Because I'm a Christian I didn't really want a Sikh wedding. However, as it was Jas's first wedding, I obliged. I couldn't take that away from him. Planning everything had been so much fun, and the wedding would be just as I'd wanted it to be. Saturday was my pre-wedding party, in a school hall near my parents' home - in fact the primary school we all attended as children. There was plenty of dancing and everyone had a good time.

Then it was the big day. I felt nervous, but in a good way. Jas texted me that morning, around 6 a.m. He said: "I love you, my baby. Today you will be all mine." It was a beautiful message and put a massive smile on my face as I was getting ready.

Our wedding day went perfectly. Luckily, it didn't snow, and even though it was cold, the sun was shining. We had a great day with all of our friends and family. It meant so much to us that they were all there, but I did miss my grandad because he had been looking forward to my wedding day. My new husband and I spent the night in a hotel, along with a bottle of champagne.

It is traditional, the day after the wedding, for the bride to go back to her parents' home with her new husband for dinner. So, my entire family:

uncles, aunts, and cousins, gathered at my mum and Dad's house to eat and talk about our fabulous wedding day. It was another big fun party.

The following morning, we went off to our honeymoon in South Africa and had a wonderful time in Cape Town, on safari and in Mauritius. In between the safari and Mauritius, we went to Johannesburg where I had arranged for us to play with lion cubs, something I had always wanted to do. I am very fond of the big cats and this experience was absolutely amazing.

Reality hit when we got back to England. So much needed doing to the house, jobs that we didn't realise at the time of purchase. We'd thought it would be a simple decorating exercise, but no, it all needed gutting and re-plastering. We spent four months renovating the house, putting in a new kitchen, a bathroom - pretty much everything was new. But it was now the way we wanted it. So that was nice. Not the ideal start to marriage that we had hoped for, but nonetheless we made the best of it and finally moved into our little haven. It was just the two of us making plans for our future, and the next big chapter in our lives would be: starting a family. We said we would wait a year, so that we could save up to have our first baby.

Chapter One

Stolen Time

The following year in October 2011, it was just amazing to see the test which said I was two to three weeks pregnant. We were so overjoyed and emotional as we had wanted this so much. We felt everything we wanted was coming together. I was quite well in the pregnancy and barely had any morning sickness. I loved being pregnant, loved my bump growing and really embraced it all.

We debated whether we wanted to know the gender of the baby, but Jas said he wasn’t sure he could keep it to himself; therefore, I knew he couldn't be trusted to find out. I knew I could keep it to myself, so at my twenty-week scan, I put a note in with my maternity chart and asked for the gender to be written down. I was delighted to find out we were having a boy as I knew Jas had always wanted a boy first.

I wasn’t actually bothered whether it was a boy or a girl, but I knew for him, being a footballer, he always wanted to teach his son his football skills.

We'd talked about names, and both liked the name Luca for a boy. I'd heard the name on a TV show, and my grandad had told me of a man he'd known years ago who was generous and kind whose name was Luca Singh.

I actually looked up the name and discovered that Luca was Italian for Luke, which meant "bringer of light". I liked that.

Throughout the pregnancy I used to say I think it's a girl, I just have this feeling, to throw Jas off. He never knew we were having a boy. It was quite fun keeping it to myself and throwing everyone off the scent when we were having conversations about the gender.

Inside I was laughing to myself and thinking, I've got a secret! We had a 3D-scan and the baby was just wonderful. He was moving his hand across his face, pulling a face and everything. It was so beautiful to see. Unfortunately, at one point the sonographer said 'he' and Jas picked up on it. I suggested maybe that was for the last couple she'd had in there, and she'd just got confused and said it again out of habit. I told him not to pay any attention to it. Again, I was laughing to myself knowing how overjoyed he would be when I gave birth to a little boy.

At one of the appointments with my midwife, she noticed that my bump was looking small. She arranged for me to have a growth scan on Friday 13th April 2012.

She laughed and said, “You're not superstitious, are you?”

I said, “A little, but I would rather know my baby’s okay, as soon as possible.”

We went to the growth scan and I was told everything was fine. The nurse kept talking about a man she knew who lived at our address before us, so we remember the appointment very well.

Everything carried on as expected for the next few weeks and I had a wonderful baby shower at my parents’ house, which was put together by my mum, sister, one of my best friends and my younger cousin. There were lots of beautiful gender-neutral gifts, and we played fabulous games that my friend organised. It was so much fun!

Before we knew it, it was the first day of my maternity leave Monday 18th June 2012. I remember the day starting so nicely. I was sitting down with a cup of tea, and Luca kicked me so hard, and I thought to myself: he's running out of room. As a big football family, I was sitting watching the football fixtures for the Premier League year ahead as they were announced on 'Sky Sports' and I was posting them on Facebook. We were getting the house ready for the baby's arrival. I had workmen in putting up blackout blinds in the bedrooms and another doing other small jobs for us. It was fair to say I was nesting.

So, the day went on and I felt the baby's flutters here and there. He always had a quiet time in the afternoon and before we knew it; it was evening. My husband came home, and I made dinner and we carried on with the evening as we always did, dinner first and then watching some TV. The Euro's 2012 football competition was taking place and, naturally, we were watching a match. Somehow Luca always knew when the football was on and he would kick more at that time. We used to laugh and say he or she is going to be a footballer. It was coming up to half time in the match and I remarked that the baby had been a little quiet that day. I thought it was strange because usually he was very active during the football. Jas brought me a cold drink to get the baby active as that had always worked previously. It didn't work this time though, so Jas brought me some chocolate, which I thought would do the trick.

"Let's wake him up," he said, " and get him to listen to the football."

This didn't work either.

I said, "I'll go upstairs to the bedroom," as that normally worked.

I suggested that the baby was probably just running out of space to move about. It was about 9:30 p.m. at this point.

I received a message from my brother, Sunny, who'd gone off to work abroad for a few weeks and he texted to say he'd arrived safely. I browsed around on my phone for a little while waiting for some movement from the little one and still there was nothing. We had been into the hospital the week before too, when I thought I had a tear in my waters as I was damp in my underwear. When we went to triage and they tested me, they'd said all was fine. Now I was getting a little concerned, so Jas suggested we call the hospital. I was still convinced it was just the baby running out of room to move.

The day before, we'd been at my parent's house as it was Father's Day, my dad's birthday, and my parent's wedding anniversary, all in one day. Luca had been really active. He was kicking, he had hiccups, and everyone had taken turns to feel my belly whilst he was moving. We laughed every time my sister put her hand on my belly, as he would stop moving - he didn't want to be active for his aunt. My sister's children were loving it and laughing, and everyone was getting excited for his arrival.

We called the hospital and they asked us to come in so they could just check to see he was okay. There was a little wait at the hospital by the time we got there so it'd probably have been around 10:30 p.m. After waiting for around twenty minutes, we were taken into a room to be monitored. The midwife connected the CTG monitor to me and brought out the scanning equipment. She began to put the gel on my tummy and started the scanning machine. She muttered about the equipment being so unpredictable at times, and that she'd get a senior midwife as she'd have better luck with the equipment.

I looked at Jas and his face was calm. The senior midwife came in and began to start scanning my tummy. There was silence and I saw the staff take a glance at each other. She asked us to bear with her whilst she went to call the doctor. I knew something was wrong and tears began to fill my eyes. Jas gripped my hand tightly as the doctor came in. He began to scan my belly and all staff looked at one another.

The doctor said the words I will never forget and that haunt me to this day, ''I'm sorry.''

I yelled out, ''No! Not my baby!''

Jas fell to his knees, holding my hand, and we sobbed in disbelief that our baby had gone. The doctor told us he would leave us for a while and then come back. He repeated how sorry he was. Jas and I just held each other and cried; we could not believe this was happening. Why was this happening?

When the doctor returned, he sat down with us. In between my tears, I asked him, ''Why has this happened? Why has my baby died?"

The doctor couldn't explain why and told us that we would need to come back in the morning to have another scan, to confirm what he'd said. We were confused and wanted to know why we had to come back to have it confirmed. He explained that the procedure was to have two scans to confirm the baby's heart had stopped and as it was nearly midnight, we would need to come back in the morning. He was very empathetic and talked to us with great sympathy. He went on to explain that I would need to deliver Luca naturally, and once he was delivered, they would check to see if there was anything wrong with the baby or with my placenta. He said he couldn't explain what might have happened, but they would do everything they could to find out what the problem was.

Jas and I went home, put our arms around each other and sobbed. Then we went to bed, but neither of us could sleep. We couldn't understand what had just happened. I was trapped in a nightmare! I then felt the need to tell Jas that we were having a boy. I didn't want him to just find out at the birth; I felt he needed to know now. I explained how long I had known and why I had kept it to myself. He hugged me and told me it didn't matter; he understood that I wanted him to have a surprise.

As the night went on, we dozed in and out of sleep not really resting, of course, just playing those words around in our heads continuously, 'I'm sorry.' The next morning, Jas had gone to the bathroom and when he came back to the bedroom I was sobbing. He held me so close and wept with me again. It was probably 7:00 a.m. and Jas needed to call his manager to explain what had happened. Just before that, we received a call from the doctor we had seen the night before, asking if we could go to the hospital for 8:00 o'clock. Jas confirmed that we could.

I told Jas that my mum knew I had an appointment that day for a check-up and she'd be calling me later to find out how it went. "You'll have to tell her now before she goes to work," I urged Jas. I also asked him to call my brother, Steven, before he went to work as I needed him with me. I'm very close to my brothers and I needed their bear hugs. Jas made the calls, first to his manager then to my mum and then Steven. It was so hard for him to make all those calls but knew he had to. Mum had already gone to work, so he decided not to tell his family just yet and wait until we came back from the hospital.

We made our way to the hospital and explained to the receptionist at triage that the doctor had asked us to come in. She said that she didn't have my name on the records and Jas explained: "We were here last night, and the doctor called this morning to ask us to come for 8:00 o'clock, so please check as he will be waiting for us." The receptionist wasted a lot of time, and we were probably waiting around for forty to fifty minutes. By this point the doctor had left and a nurse came for us. She took us to the area where I had to be scanned again to confirm that Luca's heartbeat had stopped. I was praying and hoping that they'd got it wrong and actually he was fine and just hiding from us. This was not true, however, and it was confirmed again that my baby's heart had stopped. The room was silent, except for uncontrollable sobbing from me and Jas.

I had to see a consultant next, who explained what we needed to go through over the next few days. He gave me some tablets to induce labour, and more to take later. The midwife with him explained that we could now go home and when any contractions started or if my waters broke, we should go to the hospital immediately. If that didn't happen, we were to go back to the hospital the next morning at 10 a.m. We tried to let all the information sink in as we made our way home. Jas had received some messages from my brother, Steven, and my mum. Steven had explained to his manager what had happened and that he needed to be with his sister. He was very understanding and gave my brother time off to be with me. My mum was a self-employed postmistress at this time, and she had to call the headquarters to tell them what had happened and explain that she needed to close for a couple of days.

My mum had also called my sister-in-law, Olivia, wife of my brother Sunny, asking her to get a message to Sunny to explain what had happened. Mum then had to break the news to my sister who was at work but came home immediately. Around midday, my mum, Dad and my sister came over to my home. They all put their arms around me after having hugs with Jas, and we all sobbed. My mum put her hands on my belly and questioned how this could happen as the baby had been so active on Sunday when we were at their house. She wasn't really asking the question she was just saying her thoughts out loud, trying like the rest of us to make sense of it. It was almost like she was willing him to move. After a while of the family just holding me and us all crying, we started to talk about what had happened and how it began. I explained the events of Monday night and how we had tried to get the baby moving and he simply hadn't; then going to the hospital. Meanwhile, Jas received a message from Steven explaining that he was getting a train down from London and would go to Olivia's house since she lived near the station, and they would both drive together to our house.

The day went by in quite a daze. My parents and sister left and then before we knew it, Steven and Olivia were at our home. I got that big bear hug that I needed from Steven. I sobbed into his sweatshirt and he kissed my head and cried with me. Olivia sat next to me, put her arm around me and we cried. She then told me that she had contacted Sunny's company and asked for him to be sent home. Whilst Steven and Olivia sat with me, Jas went to his parent's home to tell them the terrible news. When he came back his mum was with him and as my mum had done, she held me close and cried as she held my belly.

Jas took her back home about an hour later. Steven had said he was going to stay with us, which was a relief, because I knew he would be a great support for not just me but Jas as well. Olivia said she would go back home and wait to hear from Sunny to see when he would be able to come back. Steven made us a light dinner to keep our energy up, but none of us were really in the mood to eat.

It was Wednesday 20th June 2012. Again, I hadn't really slept. Thoughts kept going around in my head: Was it my fault? Did I do something wrong? My body had failed my child! Feelings of guilt started setting in. I kept thinking about things I should have done. Now I just wanted to give birth to my child and see him; I wanted to hold him in my arms. I wanted this next stage to be over as quickly as possible.

My hospital bags ready, we had a light breakfast and then Jas's parents and his sister came over. They wanted to see me before I went to the hospital. Jas's dad hugged me so tight and just didn't want to let go, and he cried, and I cried with him. It was the first time he'd ever hugged me like this, and I could feel the pain and the love from him. It's something I'll never forget. It felt like he wanted to wrap me in cotton wool and stop me from having to go through what was coming next. Jas's sister also did the same and said she'd be here for me, whatever I needed.

Steven took us to the hospital and Jas and I went up to the maternity ward. There was a private room ready for us. We were taken straight in and told a bereavement midwife would be along to see us shortly. I was given a gown to wear and then settled onto the bed with lots of cushions. Jas said he'd pay for the TV so that we could watch something whilst we waited for my waters to break and for labour to start. I always like watching the 'This Morning' programme, so we put that on, followed by 'Loose Women,' another one of my favourites. I was brought a jug of water and the midwives were very empathetic. They knew that I was there to give birth to my baby who had died. They ensured we were comfortable and then left us alone.

Shortly afterwards, the bereavement midwife, who was a lovely lady, arrived. She sat with us and gave us lots of information - too much to take in at the time. She spoke to us about having a post-mortem as well as an imprint of Luca's footprint and handprints in ink. She also explained that after the birth we could go to a family suite and be able to have Luca overnight. She gave us information about bereavement support that we would be able to use in the weeks to come. There was a whole packet of information, too much to go through at the time, but something we could take home. Now we just had to wait for me to deliver my baby. After about half an hour, the bereavement midwife left, and it was comforting to know that we had her to support us.

Soon it was lunchtime. There were no signs of my waters breaking or labour starting, so Jas and I were told we could go and get lunch. So we walked down to the trolley and chose something. After we'd eaten our sandwiches, Jas suggested we watch a movie together. We needed something to keep us occupied. Being big Marvel fans, we decided to watch 'Captain America'. I couldn't concentrate though, and my mind drifted into other things. I was thinking about delivering Luca and holding him. I wondered whether the labour would be easier. Then I started thinking what Luca would look like. Would he be very blue in colour? Would he look like a normal baby? I didn't know what to expect. There were so many thoughts going round and round in my head. I felt like everything was out of my control; Just not knowing what to expect. I knew that once Luca was delivered, I wanted to make sure he was dressed in his nappy and clothes, the ones that were in my hospital bag. It all left me in a daze. My head felt foggy, and I couldn't think straight - too many thoughts were making me dizzy. In the weeks to follow I realised my thoughts were quite normal.

It was now between 5:30 and 6 o'clock in the evening. We'd had some dinner and then my waters broke. Jas called for the midwife and she told us it was time to go down to the labour ward. Here goes, I thought! Almost immediately my contractions started, and they were getting stronger by the time I reached the labour ward. It seemed that within only a few minutes, I was screaming with pain. Gas and air were doing nothing for me.

The midwife asked, "Do you want an epidural?"

I yelled, "Yes!" and they went to call for an anaesthetist.

When he arrived, he tried to administer the epidural. However, it didn't work the first time, and my gosh, it was painful! I never thought I'd be one of those women who screamed in labour, but I was. The anaesthetist tried to administer it again, and again, but it didn't work. After six attempts and whilst I was screaming with pain, Jas was getting angry and worried. The midwife recommended they call a senior anaesthetist; I had no idea we had a junior one. Was I not going through enough giving birth to my sleeping child, now I have a junior who couldn't even administer an epidural?! What on earth were they thinking? The senior anaesthetist promptly arrived and administered the epidural all in one quick go. The seventh attempt had worked.

After having about four or five people in the room with us whilst the epidural was being administered, we were now just down to the midwife - the midwife who stayed with us throughout my labour. She was fantastic. She explained to me that because I'd had the epidural, I would not feel the contractions, so she would check regularly to see how dilated I was and how strong the contractions were. I lay back on my bed waiting for nature to take its course. The farce with the epidural had made me feel quite poorly and unfortunately my earlier dinner came up.

By around 8:30 p.m. I was willing Luca to come out. The next day would be the birthdays of my sister-in-law, Olivia, and Jas's eldest nephew. I was thinking that they didn't really need to be sharing their birthday with Luca, who was never going to be here to celebrate his birthday alongside them. When you are always caring about others, it's strange how your mind thinks – even when you're giving birth to your stillborn baby.

As these thoughts were going around in my head, nothing was really happening in terms of contractions and dilation, and it felt like I was waiting forever.

Because I was on the main labour ward, I could hear the cries of mothers giving birth and babies being born, and It broke my heart knowing that my baby was going to come out of my body, the body that had nurtured and loved him from inception, and I would never hear his cry. It was so hard. Not that I begrudged other women having their babies; quite the contrary, it was just hard knowing I was not going to hear my baby's beautiful newborn sounds.

The midwife came in and out throughout the night to see if I had dilated any more. I had. She thought she'd seen Luca's hand, so went to get a doctor to check if this was going to make delivery problematic. It was the same doctor who had pronounced Luca dead on Monday night. It was good to know that we were in safe hands as he was a really nice doctor. He checked and everything was okay, so it would be a normal delivery. He continued to speak with Jas and I and sat with us for a while. He asked us why we hadn't arrived early on Tuesday, and we explained we had but that the receptionist had been extremely adamant that we had no appointment. He then wanted to know which receptionist, what she looked like etc. I didn't know her name but described her. The doctor rolled his eyes as if to say that they'd had lots of problems with this particular receptionist in the past. He said that he'd be having words with her.

He then reiterated that after I'd delivered our son, they would be looking for signs of anything that may have caused his death. This could be the cord wrapped around his neck, which was the most common reason. They would also look at my placenta to see if there were any blockages or clots that could be signs of why Luca had passed. The doctor said that the next option, if all was okay, was to have a post-mortem. Jas and I had already decided we wanted to do this. We needed to know why our baby had died.

Our kind doctor then started talking about the future and the different levels of grieving that we would go through. The anger we'd display, the acceptance, the continuing grief. He said that if we decided to have children in the future, that I'd be monitored a lot more closely and they would ensure I had an obstetrician that I felt comfortable with. He said there were a number of great obstetricians at the hospital, and he mentioned a few of them. He said there was one lady who scanned at every appointment and there was another who would take care of me in other ways. I knew when he mentioned the obstetrician who did regular scans, that she was definitely the one I wanted. Obviously at this point I wasn't really thinking about having another child, I was just concerned about delivering my child now and holding him in my arms for as long as I could. After sitting with us for about forty minutes, the doctor was called to another patient and he wished us all the best, under the circumstances. It had just gone midnight; Jas and I were drifting in and out of sleep constantly. It was also hard to sleep, of course, as it was a noisy labour ward.

Then, around 7:15 a.m. on 21 June 2012, I was fully dilated, and my contractions were stronger. So the lovely midwife, who had been with us all night long, said that it was time to deliver our baby. Another midwife came in and explained she was going to assist with the delivery. I couldn't feel my contractions because of the epidural, so they explained that they would monitor when my contractions were happening and then tell me to push. It felt like I was pushing for ages. In reality it was probably twenty minutes, certainly not much longer. Jas held my hand and supported me whilst I was pushing. The midwife encouraged me to give one last big push. Jas held my hand and said, 'Come on, baby, you can do this!' I pushed again, giving it all I had. Then the midwife said, "He's here."

There was an awful silence, and both Jas and I

cried. The midwife who had been with us all night should have been off duty by now, but God bless her, she stayed as she wanted to be there when I delivered Luca.

"He's beautiful," she said, and she showed him to me.

My gosh, yes, he was just beautiful. I didn't hold him straight away. I still had that thing in my head, that I needed him in his clothes and his nappy. But It wasn't as if I was having the normal skin to skin contact with him which I would have done ordinarily. So, it was a strange thought. Maybe I was thinking that if he was dressed then he'd be okay, and I'd be able to take him home. The second midwife now took over and explained that she'd get him cleaned up for us and then bring him back. In the meantime, they were preparing to remove my placenta but were having difficulty. It seemed to be stuck, so they called the doctor. I thought this was why my baby had passed - that there was something wrong with my placenta. Another doctor tried to detach the placenta, but couldn't, and told me I would need to go to theatre for it to be done.

I asked, "Is this normal? Is this why my son has

passed?"

The doctor replied, "This does happen sometimes, but it's not a reason why a baby would pass."

However, she explained that when they took my placenta out, they would be checking it for clots and blockages.

Whilst they were getting things ready for me to go to theatre, I suggested that Jas might want to have some time with Luca. He said he would like that. He was also going to call our parents to let them know that Luca had been delivered and tell them when they could visit. I was wheeled off to theatre to get the placenta detached and removed. The midwife had been called to another mother in labour, but she assured me that Luca would be with us soon. When the placenta was removed, they checked it and found no blockages or clots. I asked what would happen next, and they told me they would send the placenta to be examined more thoroughly. Clearly it wasn't my placenta that had failed Luca, so what could it be?

I was taken back to the labour ward and Jas was

waiting in the room.

"Where's Luca?" I asked.

His eyes were red. I wasn't sure whether he'd been crying or whether it was from lack of sleep.

I asked again: "What's the matter, Jas? Where's Luca?"

"I'm not sure," he replied,

I said, "Haven't you asked anyone?"

He said, "Yes. I went out to call our parents and then came back hoping Luca would be here, but as he wasn't, I went out to the desk and asked if I could have him."

He breathed deeply and explained that the midwife at the desk, an Asian lady, had asked him if he was the father of the dead baby?

In utter shock, I gasped and said, "She said what?!!"

Clearly Jas had been crying because of this most insensitive woman who clearly was in the wrong job if she could say such unkind words. I choked up thinking what he must have felt when she said that to him - the same way I was now feeling having heard it. How can anyone in the nursing profession be so vile and insensitive with their words. I just could not comprehend this.

By now we were watching the clock, wondering where on earth Luca was. Every time a midwife came by, we asked if we could have our son. Each time we got the reply: “Yes, I’ll see what I can do.” It was now lunchtime, so we had sandwiches, and a cup of tea whilst we waited for our son. I had given birth to him just after 8 o'clock and it was now after lunchtime and he still wasn’t with us. Where was he? I was becoming more and more frustrated. We had been left alone now for a couple of hours. Jas had gone out to the desk again, but no one was there for him to ask. So, we just waited and waited and waited. It was ridiculous. This was precious time we should have been having with our son, and he wasn’t even with us.

Around 4 p.m., our bereavement midwife came in to see us. The first thing I said to her was that we hadn’t seen Luca since this morning, when I delivered him. She was shocked and said she’d go and find out what was happening and where he was. She came back a few minutes later. Apparently, he was in the room next door, and the pediatricians were with him checking him over. She said she'd go and make copies of Luca's handprints and footprints whilst they checked him. All this time – it had been eight hours - and my baby had been laying there in the next room whilst we were elsewhere waiting for him, and nobody was able to bring him to us. What on earth had they been doing? Surely if they knew he was next door they could have just wheeled him into the room for us? It would have taken them less than a minute to do it, and eight hours later we now find this out! We were fuming, and just couldn't believe that our child had been treated in such a way. Within half-an-hour, the bereavement midwife wheeled Luca into our room in his cot. Finally, our son was with us!

She took him out of the cot and placed our baby in my arms. I smiled at him, he was beautiful and then I wept. Jas touched his head and kissed him. He was perfect, there was nothing wrong with him that we could see. I asked the bereavement midwife what the pediatricians had said. She told us that they had measured him and checked him over but there was nothing that they could find wrong with him. She said he really was a beautiful boy, and I nodded in agreement. Then she said: “Now let me go and find out if we can get you up to a family room; then you can call your family to come and meet Luca, once you've settled.” At this point I thought there's no way you're taking our baby out of my arms since it's taken nearly nine hours for us to have him back. Jas wanted to hold Luca, so I gently passed him over. There was a blood stain on his nose and the bereavement midwife explained it would have been caused when the pediatricians were checking him. This made me feel like he was very fragile, so I was extra careful when passing him to Jas. He wept as he held our first child, Luca, in his arms - our son, who from the moment of conception was a much wanted and loved baby. The midwife came back and said that the family room was ready for us and they said they’d take me up in a wheelchair. I asked to hold Luca, but she said she would place him in a Moses basket and bring him up to the room once we were there. I made it clear that as our time with Luca had been made shorter by the incompetence of the staff not bringing him to us, I didn’t want to wait any longer and for there to be any more delays. She assured me it would be soon after we’d arrived in the family room.

My wheelchair was brought around, and I was helped into it. I held a memory box that we had been given to keep Luca's things in. Jas carried the bags, and we were taken up to a ward. We had to go past the main reception in triage just outside the labour ward. There were lots of parents and expectant mums sitting there looking at us as we went by. Clearly they could see that we'd been crying, but they had no idea what we had been going through. When we got up to the ward, we were taken into the family room. It had a double bed, a TV, and en suite. It was almost like a hotel room really. Jas had called our families telling them that they could now come to the hospital and gave them the ward information. Luca was a little blue in the lips and around his face and for some reason I felt like I needed to tell my family this, so they didn't feel shocked when they saw him. Again, thinking about other people's feelings, but you can't change natural instincts. I texted my brother, Steven, and asked him to tell everybody that Luca was a little bit blue so they wouldn't be too shocked. I didn't know what they'd really be expecting. As we settled down, I looked at the room and thought to myself, why could I not have given birth to Luca in this room. It was private and away from the labour ward, that way I would not have had to hear all the other babies being born and crying!

Jas's parents and his sister arrived first. Luca wasn't in the room by this point, so they sat and waited and asked me how it had been. The door then opened, and the midwife came in with Luca in a Moses basket. My mother-in-law was the first one to get up to look at Luca, and she smiled and said he looked like my brother, Steven. Obviously if he looked like Steven that meant he looked like me, I thought. Tears filled her eyes - this was her first grandson from her eldest son, but there was no joy, just heartbreak at the thought that he had died. Jas's sister wanted to take a couple of photos to show her sons, and I said that was fine; she also said how gorgeous he was. Within a few minutes my family had arrived: my parents, Steven, my sister and my grandma, who I called “nanny”, who was Luca's only remaining great grandparent. The first thing she did was hold me in her arms and I wept on her shoulder. My parents cried as they looked at Luca. My mum said he was perfect and gorgeous. The families paid their condolences to each other whilst in the room and then everyone just looked at Luca. Conversations went on, but I'm not really sure what they were about, I can't remember. One thing I do remember though is that as they were talking, no one took their eyes off Luca. My mom sat next to me on the bed and held my hand, showing me the love you can only get from your mother. I could feel it just by holding hands.

At around 7:30 p.m. Jas's family left but my family said they would stay until 8 p.m. which was the end of normal visiting hours. My dad took some photos of Luca and then he asked if he could hold him. I really wanted to say yes, but knowing that his nose had bled earlier, I said, "I think he's a bit fragile", and explained what had happened earlier. He said, "Okay, don't worry." My mum spoke to Luca saying how delighted and excited they were when they knew that I was having him. She was crying whilst holding my hand and talking to Luca. It was the grief she was feeling for the loss of Luca, but I knew it was because of what I was going through too. 8:00 p.m. came and my family had to leave. Each one of them gave Luca a kiss on his head knowing that they wouldn't see him again. I asked my sister to call two of my best friends to inform them of what had happened, and she said she would. My family hugged Jas and I, and Mum said that I should try and get some sleep. I know that I must have had massive bags under my eyes from the lack of sleep and obviously from crying with grief for my son. Before leaving, Mum told me that my brother Sunny had also arrived, but that he'd come to see us tomorrow if that was okay. I was pleased and said, "That'd be lovely."

Now it was just the three of us: Jas, Luca and me. I took Luca out of his Moses basket and held him close, then Jas held him, and we took it in turns a couple of times. A midwife came in to give me some painkillers, as understandably, I had a horrible headache. She asked Jas if he was okay, and if he needed any Paracetamol; he said he was okay. She brought us a jug of water and then left us for the night. She said if we needed anything, we should just press the buzzer. I placed Luca back into the Moses basket and went to the bathroom to put my pyjamas on, brush my teeth and pass urine for the first time that day, as I'd had a catheter in all this time. I went back into my room and lay down and Jas lay next to me, holding me close whilst we both just looked at Luca. "Time to get some sleep. We're both exhausted." I said, and Jas agreed. So we dimmed the lights and fell asleep.

On Friday, 22 June 2012, we woke up at around 7:30 a.m. I had been waking during the night, checking on Luca. How strange, but my mother's instinct had already crept in, and I was doing what was natural between a mother and her baby. But what was I really checking on? He wasn't alive. However, that didn't stop me from waking up and looking at the still body of my baby. Perhaps I was hoping for a miracle.

After breakfast the midwife came in and said they would give us a couple more hours with our baby and someone would come to speak to us about signing the post-mortem forms. A couple of hours is that all? Is that really all we have with Luca? I couldn't believe it. The day before, the day of his birth, it had taken us nearly nine hours to get him back with us. Yes, we'd had him overnight, but we were sleeping…and now, just a couple more hours? I took Luca out of the Moses basket knowing these final hours were going to be so precious and nowhere near enough. I walked around with him. Again, that motherly instinct, that feeling, was making me do things that didn't really make sense. I was rocking him in my arms and didn't even realise it. But clearly the natural mother within me needed to do this; after all, that's what mother's do. It felt so nice holding Luca in my arms and rocking him, as if he was alive. It was somehow nurturing for me, and I hoped his spirit felt nurtured too.

The midwife came back In and I asked why we could only have a couple of hours with my baby, and she replied that it was because his body would deteriorate if he wasn't put in a cold container. Woah, a cold container? These were words I did not like hearing, but unfortunately, this was our reality. I knew she was right, since I had noticed there was a slight odour coming from Luca's mouth. It wasn't horrible, but I understood that it would become worse over time, even over hours. It just didn't feel fair! It had taken us so long to get him back with us, through no fault of our own but because the staff on the labour ward had ignored us. Now we needed to make the most of these two hours. Jas and I took it in turns holding Luca, and I took a few photos of him in his Moses basket looking sound asleep. His skin was clearing a bit today and he wasn't looking quite so blue. He was gorgeous. My grandma had said the night before he was too gorgeous for this world and maybe she was right, but it didn't soften the blow. In my head all I could think about was holding him for as long as I could, even though we knew we hadn't got very long. I asked Jas if I should take a photo of Luca in his arms, and he said, "If you do, when I look back at the photos, it'll make me cry.'

At times like this, when you're told you've only got a couple of hours with your child, a child that you're never going to see again, the child that you love with all your heart, you can't really think clearly. All we thought about was just holding him. Whilst I held Luca for the last time, a doctor came in and wanted to go through the paperwork for the post-mortem. We listened and then he said he'd leave the paperwork and come back later when we'd had a chance to read through it.

It was almost 10 o'clock when the midwife came in and said, "Shall we take him?"

I nodded, but inside I was saying NO, not yet. I held Luca tight against my chest so that I could smell his hair and kiss his head. I could feel the anxiety building inside me because I didn't want to let him go. I kept thinking: they're going to take my baby soon. He's my baby! This isn't how things should be. Mother Nature has gone wrong! Horribly wrong! I should be looking forward to taking my son home now, not dreading them taking him to the mortuary.

Twenty minutes passed, the midwife came again and asked, “Are you ready now?”

I shook my head and said, “No!”

Jas could see that I was not going to let her take Luca, and that I would keep delaying them.

He said, “Shaz, we’re going to have to let them take him. I know we don't want to, but we will have to.”

I nodded my head in agreement, not that I really agreed at all. I was really thinking, this just isn't long enough to spend with our baby. I can't let him go now. But I had no choice. It felt as if my heart was being ripped out of my body with all the pain I was feeling having to let go of my son. The anxiety was already building, and my breathing was getting heavier. I didn't want to do this!

“I’m not going to see him again,” I said to Jas.

“I know, baby. This is going to be very hard.”

We had Luca for another twenty minutes or so and I held him, kissing him all over - his hands, his head, his cheeks, even his cute little button nose, and then finally a little kiss on his lips. I told him that I was always going to be his mummy and promised him he would live on as long as I was alive; that his name and his memory would stay alive. Jas had his arm around me and a hand on Luca; he kissed his cheeks and said, "I love you, my baby boy." We both cried knowing that these were the last few moments we had with our baby.

"I can't do this," I told Jas. "How am I going to give him up? We won't see him again."

I was crying so much I was finding it hard to get my words out. Through <u>his</u> tears, Jas said:

"I know, babe, that we're never going to see Luca again, but let's remember his face, his little hands and hug him tight now."

Then he held and hugged both Luca and I close to him as the door opened. There was the mid-wife again asking if she could take our baby now. I didn't reply but Jas nodded. Before I placed Luca in his Moses basket, I gave him one last hug, kissed his head and his cheeks again and said, "I love you with all my heart, my baby boy, and always will."

Then I broke down in tears as the midwife carried Luca away. "My baby! No! My baby!!" Jas threw his arms around me and we sat on the bed sobbing and sobbing uncontrollably together.

After ten minutes or so the doctor came back for the post-mortem forms. I told him that we hadn't really read them, and he said, "That's okay, I've explained everything anyway."

Jas had a glance over the forms and agreed. We both signed them and asked how long it would take. The doctor explained it varied, but for a baby it shouldn't be too long. He said they would keep in contact with our funeral directors and let them know when our son would arrive after the post-mortem.

Jas called Steven and asked him to come and pick us up. As I put things in my bag, the midwife came in and we told her that we'd be going home now. She said she understood, and then handed me some tablets to take. She also explained that a midwife would be in contact with me as I would still need to be checked at home just like any new mother. Wow, I wasn't really expecting that.

She said it was standard procedure to visit mothers who had recently given birth.

Steven had parked his car close to the hospital entrance doors and as soon as we got in the car, he drove off. As we were leaving, I looked back at the hospital through the rear window, and my eyes filled with tears. I was leaving the hospital without my baby who'd been taken to the mortuary. I cried and Jas put his hand around mine. When we arrived home, I cried thinking about the fact that I was walking into my house without my baby boy. I felt so empty. This was not the way things should have been.

Shortly after arriving home, there was a knock at the door. It was a delivery. Gosh, what timing. The delivery was the travel system we had ordered for Luca: his pushchair, and his car seat with the ISOFIX. Jas asked the delivery guy to place the things in our converted garage. The gentleman said, "You're going to have your hands full soon." Jas gave him a weak smile and thanked him for the delivery. His heart was breaking seeing everything we had ordered for Luca being delivered, but he couldn't say: "Actually, no, our baby died." I had forgotten those baby items were arriving. Everything just felt so unfair. Why had this happened? I felt like I was living in an endless nightmare. Jas came back in and put his arm around me and we both shed more tears.

My mum had messaged to say that she was going to pop in and see me and bring some food. My brother Sunny and his wife were also coming and my sister and her family too. When Sunny arrived, he gave me a big bear hug and I wept in his arms. He kissed my forehead and said, “I'm so sorry, sis.” Soon my mum, my sister and her family arrived. Our small house was suddenly full of people but not the person that I wanted the most, Luca. I was in a daze. Conversations were happening around me, but I wasn't present. It felt as if I was on another planet - a planet of grief, confusion, emptiness, hurt. I was heartbroken, something completely unknown to me. Suddenly I was back in the room and my nephew was laughing at something my brother, Sunny, had said. My nephew had a cute loud laugh, which was pleasant to hear, although at this time in particular it felt strange. I was exhausted and suddenly felt a headache coming on, so I told everyone that I needed to lie down. I asked my mum if they could all come back the following day. I felt a little bad saying this as I know my family's actions and thoughts were only in my interest, but it was really a little too soon to have everyone together. Mum understood and said, "It's okay, my sweetheart. I wasn't sure whether it would help to have us all or not. We'll come again tomorrow, and I'll make you something different to eat, but I've left enough lasagna for you to have tonight." She knew that was my favourite. They all gave me huge hugs and went on their way. Sunny said he'd be in contact whilst he was away and told me to take care, and that he loved me.

The following day, Jas's parents came to visit, and his mum also brought us food. They sat for a while, as they did several times over the next few weeks. As the days went on, we received messages of condolence and kind words from lots of people. Several close friends and cousins visited during the next few weeks as we waited for the news that Luca's body had been released from the post-mortem. Then we could set his funeral date. Whilst waiting to organise the funeral, I couldn't stop the thoughts from going around in my head, asking the same question: what had I done wrong? How did I fail my baby? I wasn't sleeping very well, and a rash had broken out all over my body and on my face. It looked like an allergic reaction to the medication I'd been given, or perhaps something I'd eaten, so Jas drove me to see the doctor.

When I sat down, the doctor said, "Oh you don't look over thirty-six weeks pregnant."

Jas and I just looked at one another, then he told her our baby was stillborn. I began to cry, and she said she was so sorry. She hadn't been informed. I assumed that my GP would have been informed of our tragic loss; shouldn't that have been the normal procedure? Yet she had no idea. I wondered whether this was a failure in the system or just the way things were. Maybe I was just focusing on these things to try and make things easier for myself, trying to get my head around it all. The doctor spoke for a while about bereavement, and I explained the reason I'd gone in to see her that day. I think she could tell from my eyes I hadn't been sleeping, so she gave me some light sleeping pills, which I had for a week to ten days. They helped me sleep and to get my body used to a new timetable. I couldn't face going to the chemist for my prescription, so Jas went for me. Since the people in the chemist knew me very well, I asked Jas to tell them that Luca had passed away. When he came back, he said they were utterly shocked, and cried. They'd also sent their regards to me.

Our closest friends came to visit us. One said, "I don't know what to say!" Jas replied, "The fact you're here, says it all for us." There were many more visitors over the coming weeks, and we received lovely messages. It was comforting to see how much support and love we had from our family and friends. Many didn't know what to say, but the fact that they were there, meant a lot to us.

Two weeks after my son had died, someone delivered a wedding invitation to our house. My thoughts were: do you seriously think I'm going to dress up for a wedding when my son has just died? I felt like screaming ARE YOU SERIOUS?! But no, I kept quiet, but I was raging inside. Apparently, the groom's parents had insisted we had the invitation, in case by then I was up to going. I wanted to shout: ERM…NO!!

I barely left the house for weeks. I just couldn't face people and the outside world. I was feeling increasingly lonely and felt as if I had a big hole inside. My arms wanted to be holding my baby, but instead they were empty. I constantly thought of what I would be doing if Luca had been alive. I was growing increasingly depressed and cried every day.

My brother, Steven, started a baby charity and began fundraising in Luca's memory. Our neighbours, friends, and family all donated money, and over £1,500 was raised.

Summary

If you are taken to the labour ward to give birth to your 'sleeping' baby, then ask (insist) on being taken to the bereavement family room to give birth, away from all the heartbreak of hearing the cry of other babies being born.

It's very important at this stage, whether you are in the family room or any other room, to ask for a cuddle cot if it has not already been offered. This equipment will gift you the extra time you need to say goodbye to your little angel baby.

From this first chapter, I would like you to understand the key points I am trying to make as I tell my story. The mother of a stillborn will still have motherly instincts and her post-pregnancy body.

This will make her feel increasingly depressed, empty, and lonely. When I say lonely, I mean loneliness because she is without her baby, not loneliness because people aren't around her.

There will be anger, grief, feelings of being stuck in a nightmare, heartache, tears, suicidal thoughts, anxiety, wanting to be alone, wanting people with you, fear, anguish, and much more, but know that these are perfectly normal reactions to the loss of your child, and you are certainly not alone in these feelings.

If you are someone supporting a mother and father who have suffered the loss of a baby, please put yourself in their shoes. It's hard to imagine losing your child, but if you are a parent, just try and picture the horror and trauma of your child passing away before he/she is born. Think of the insensitive words that could cause pain, and please don't say them to the Angel Warrior you are supporting. Understand that at times the bereaved parents will be wanting to talk, sometimes not wanting to talk. It might appear that they're back to 'normal', but know that they will never be the same people they were. You will be supporting their new normal. Give them a shoulder to cry on; let them feel they can talk openly, and just listen. You don't always have to respond. Sit in silence with them – perhaps just watching television together.

Do not say:

1. It was meant to be.
2. It's part of God's plan.
3. You're healthy, so you can have another child.
4. At least you have other children.
5. When will you have another baby?
6. You need to move on, look to the future.
7. You need to get out.
8. Have faith.
9. You'll get over it.

Support these grieving parents, whether it be the mother or the father, with suggestions, such as:

1. Would you like to go out?
2. Shall I make you some food?

3. Let's have a cup of tea and just sit and watch television, shall we?
4. What would you like to do?
5. Is there anything I can help you with?
6. Can I do the ironing? Or is there anything else that needs doing around the house?

Simply be helpful.

Chapter Two

So hard to say goodbye

We were now getting ready for the funeral after ordering flower arrangements - one that spelled out "SON", which was, of course, from Jas and I, and one that said "LUCA". This one was collectively from the family – Luca's aunts, uncles, grandparents, and cousins. We didn't really want too many flowers for his tiny coffin, so we decided just to do it like that. There was no point in having separate flowers from the younger members of the family, so we just chose the two special arrangements.

A couple of weeks earlier when Luca's body had been released from the post-mortem, we were able to set the date of the funeral, 17th July 2012. When we were at the funeral home, we collected the clothes that Luca wore in hospital. I was horrified that my baby's little hat was soaked with blood. "Why is there so much blood? I asked the lady at the funeral home. "As part of the post-mortem they had to cut his head open to assess his brain,' she responded, very matter-of-factly. I shivered with despair knowing what my baby son's body had been put through, and I cried. I couldn't get the image out of my head, and it haunts me to this day.

When we were back home, I washed Luca's clothes, and since it was a rainy day I laid them out on the dining room chairs to dry. It was then I noticed that his little baby grow onesie had a heart shaped blood stain on the left-hand side, just where his heart would have been. In that moment I felt it was a message of love from Luca, and I hugged the onesie tightly. I still do this every now and again, and it gives me great comfort.

It seemed that the only time I went out of the house was to go with Jas to arrange Luca's funeral. The pouring out of sympathy from the people we met was very apparent. You could see on their faces that they were thinking, 'this poor couple; what must they be going through.' We were going through hell. It's the kind of journey that you never ever expect to go on; the life experience you never think you can actually deal with, but somehow, we had to. Believe me, it wasn't easy, and it still isn't, but you learn to just take it day by day. I couldn't tell anyone what was going on in my head, as they wouldn't really understand. At times, all I wanted to do was scream, shout and cry with sorrow and anger.

I was broken and not feeling like a person anymore - more like a zombie, just going through the motions. Everything looked grey. There was no colour in the world for me anymore. I couldn't hear the birds; the sun would shine, but I didn't feel it's warmth. Life had lost all meaning.

Some days Jas needed to get out, and I understood that, so he'd go and play golf with one of his best friends. As much as I hated being left alone at home, I knew he needed that release and that it would be good for him. Whilst he was out, I thought about what my newborn baby, Luca, would be doing if he were here. He'd probably be sleeping or perhaps I'd have him in my arms and feeding him from my breasts. However, since I'd been given medication to stop the flow of milk, this was another part of being a mother to Luca that I missed - the intimacy of breast-feeding. I was always thinking about the things I would have been doing if my baby were here, instead of the nothingness that filled me.

As the funeral approached, I don't really know what I was feeling, apart from the fact it wasn't how I wanted to be feeling. The night before the funeral I was very anxious. I had every right to be grieving and crying at my son's funeral, but I suppose I was worried I would collapse completely. I wondered if I was going to be able to say my final goodbye to my son. I wasn't ready. I just couldn't do it! I knew I couldn't see him because the funeral directors had already told us that his body would have deteriorated quite a bit. But I couldn't put it off forever - the day was set and everything was in place. I felt sick and just wanted to curl up in a corner and die rather than have to go to my own son's funeral. I still had all those doubts in my head about what I had done wrong, and how I had failed my son. I felt it should have been me in the coffin, not him. It wasn't fair! What had we ever done to deserve this kind of pain? A pain that is so deep, it cuts through every fibre of your being and it feels as if your heart has been ripped apart. Our world had been thrown upside down in the most unimaginable way.

On the morning of the funeral, I decided to wear one of my maternity tunics. It was in pastel colours, and as the weather was quite warm, I wore it with black leggings and a long black cardigan. I had been so comfortable in the tunic when I was pregnant with Luca, and I almost imagined I could feel him moving around in my stomach. It was an eerie sensation, but also quite calming.

Our two families began to arrive at our house and I sensed that they were all feeling quite anxious. None of us had ever been to a funeral for a baby. There was almost a quiet hush in the room until the funeral car, with Luca's coffin inside, pulled up outside. Jas and I had already agreed that he would carry Luca's coffin into the house. In a way, it was the last time he was ever going to carry his son. As I saw him approaching the front door carrying Luca's casket, I burst into uncontrollable tears. Our son shouldn't be coming home for the first time in a box. He should have been in our arms when we arrived home after his birth.

The funeral driver laid out a stand on which Luca's coffin could sit. Jas came over to me after laying down Luca's casket, and we both sobbed in each other's arms whilst everyone else sobbed too. After a short while, Jas's dad asked if they should leave us alone with our son, and we nodded. Everyone made their way outside and stood on our driveway whilst Jas and I sat next to Luca's coffin. We each put one hand on his coffin and held hands with the other. We spoke to him about how active he always was in this room, especially when the football was on. We told him it would be the last time he'd be in here, but it was his favourite room by far. We told him about all the plans that we'd had for him when he came home, and how he should have been alive in our arms. I told him about the baby gifts and the car seat that had been delivered for him, that he could not use. I promised I would always keep his name and memory alive, and that this was never going to be goodbye forever because one day we would meet again in the hereafter. I told him that I didn't want to say goodbye, it was too hard for me to do and that I just wanted to tell him that I would always love and miss him, and that a piece of my heart was going with him.

Just as I finished saying that, Jas's dad came into the room and asked if we were ready to go. We told him we were and that we had said everything that we could. The driver of the funeral car carried out Luca's coffin and someone else packed up the stand. As I walked out of my house, my dad put his arm around me and walked me to the funeral car. When it's a baby's funeral you don't get a hearse, it's just a funeral car. I got into the back and was followed by Jas and then my mum. Luca's casket was passed to us so that we could hold him all the way to the crematorium. His flowers were put behind us and could be seen out of the windows. His other three grandparents sat in front of us. Everyone else made their way in their own cars. I could see the shapes of my neighbours looking at us from a distance, as we drove off.

We had chosen a couple of songs that felt right for us, and as we reached the crematorium, the doors opened, and the Ed Sheeran song 'Little Bump' was playing. The funeral director carried Luca's coffin into the chapel, and we followed behind. He then placed the tiny coffin onto a large table as we all took our seats. The funeral was conducted by the hospital chaplain who spoke so beautifully about our special little boy. He said that our baby had made a mark on our lives, even though he had not breathed our air. Then followed with: "His existence will never be forgotten." These words could not have been truer. As the chaplain finished, he encouraged us to say our final goodbyes whilst music played in the background. Jas and I held hands and walked towards Luca. I put my arms around his coffin and lay my head on top of it. I sobbed as I said to my little boy, "This is it now, son. You've got to go even though I don't want you to. I love you so much and if crying could bring you back, you would already be back by now."

I kissed his coffin a few times, Jas did the same. We both sobbed our hearts out and could see some of the family doing the same. I couldn't take my arms off his coffin because I knew that would be the last time I'd be holding him, albeit he was in his casket. Eventually, Jas had to tell me to let go. I refused, saying I didn't want to. So he held me for a short while as I put my head on Luca's coffin again.

I said, "Bye for now, my beautiful boy. I will see you again one day. I will always be your mummy and you will always be my first baby." Then I kissed his coffin again for the last time.

Jas and I walked to our seats. I nodded to let Luca's grandparents know they could now say their goodbyes too, which they did.

The chaplain gave me a look as if to ask if it was okay, and I nodded. The curtain closed around Luca's coffin, and then he was out of sight. I felt my heart break into more pieces. My legs felt like jelly and I held onto Jas. There are no words for the magnitude of pain you feel at your child's funeral.

We walked out slowly. Luca's special flowers from the family had been placed against the wall outside the chapel, including flowers from friends, and everyone took their time to read the cards attached. We shook hands with the chaplain and thanked him for a lovely service. The driver of the funeral car was ready to take us on to our next destination, a Sikh temple. Because Jas' family are Sikh, they had arranged for some prayers at a small temple. On arrival at the temple, the relatives gave us hugs of condolence. As we listened to the priest's words, we realised that he had not taken on board the fact that Luca had not taken a breath in this world. His speech and prayer assumed that he had, which I found quite disappointing.

After having something to eat, we made our way

back home with my family. Jas's family stayed on at the temple. I wanted to go to Coventry Cathedral and light candles for Luca. Everyone said it was a good idea, so we all went together. I spent a little time alone on one side of the cathedral just saying my own prayers about the day. I thanked God for giving me the strength I'd needed and prayed that He would walk with me as I carried on through more dark days to come.

Around this time 'Rihanna' released her song 'Diamonds.' I loved it immediately and started changing the words. In my head, I sang:

'Shine bright, tonight, Luca…you're beautiful, my diamond in the sky.'

That's how I saw Luca now, my diamond in the sky.

This has been my song ever since, and it's my ringtone on my phone too.

* * * * * * * * * * *

Jas had another two weeks off work. In total he had six weeks off with me, which was very good of his company. In those two weeks, however, it became quite obvious that people were expecting us to move on now that we'd had Luca's funeral. For instance, we'd been invited to a party the following month, but needless to say, we were not in any sort of party mood.

As much as family and friends were trying to be understanding of our grief, I know they were also anxious for us to "move on", which I felt was for their sake as well as ours. If Jas and I had gone to the party, it would have been awkward for all of us. They would feel guilty about celebrating and having fun in front of us, and we would have put a damper on everything. But we couldn't pretend to be happy, especially if it was just to make them feel more comfortable. It was a difficult situation for everyone. We couldn't stop them from living their lives, but we wouldn't be ready to 'move on' with our lives for a very long time. If fact you never move on, you find a new normal eventually!

In the end, we declined invitations to parties and special occasions, but then we found out that one of Jas's good friends had welcomed a baby boy and didn't even text Jas to tell him the good news. Either he felt guilty and didn't want to share the news with Jas because of the loss of our baby, or he didn't want to spoil their special time. Jas took this quite hard, as ordinarily his friend would have told him immediately. It felt as if we were in our own sort of bubble, and no-one could talk to us and especially share good news about their lives with us. This was particularly hard because we have always been happy for others. Then suddenly we were being pushed away just as if we were aliens.

A relative also got married shortly after that, and even though we didn't attend, the rest of my family were obliged to go. I knew they weren't really in the mood for a celebration as they were still grieving, but nonetheless they put on their best smiles and carried on. They were still obviously happy for my cousin, as we all were, we just were not quite ready to party.

Jas and I did what we could to support each other, and we cried a lot. One day I was sobbing uncontrollably, and Jas asked what he could do to help. I shouted that the only thing that would help was to bring my baby back.

"Can you bring him back? That's what I need. I don't need anything else; I just need my baby! Can you do that for me?" I yelled.

Of course, he couldn't, so I shouted some more, "Then there's nothing you can do for me, so just leave me alone!"

I wasn't angry at Jas, of course. It wasn't his fault our son had died. He was mourning too. I snapped because all I really wanted was my baby. If anyone else asked me if they could do anything to help, my thought was always the same: all I wanted was my baby back - that's what they could do for me. Obviously, I knew they couldn't bring Luca back, but that's all I needed at that time; there wasn't anything else. I didn't need anyone saying that 'it would be okay in time', or 'time is a healer' or anything else along those lines. All I needed was my baby. Why didn't people just get that?

Then Jas went back to work and I was all alone at home. He would call quite often during the day, just to check how I was. Sometimes I'd be crying, and he felt helpless. The first few days, and particularly the day he returned to work, people were asking him how I was; they weren't asking how he was, although he had also lost his son. The bereavement midwife had warned us that people would ask about me more than Jas, and that was indeed the case.

One day I got a text message from my aunt. She'd just heard that Gary Barlow's daughter was stillborn and wondered how I was feeling about this since it was all over the news. Of course, I was heartbroken for Gary and his wife. I also wondered if this might help break the stigma of stillborn baby loss since I'd already learned that there was a big taboo around discussing this kind of baby loss. Although I knew it'd happened in the past to other celebrities, such as Amanda Holden, I just thought that maybe Gary Barlow would do something to break the silence on this. I felt for them so much. I knew they would be struggling in the first initial dark period and that, unfortunately, there would be many more dark days ahead. If I remember correctly, Gary Barlow was working on 'X Factor' at this time and the live shows would be starting a month after the loss of his child. I wondered if he would pull out during this time of grieving or whether he would put on a mask, as so many do, and carry on with his job. That's exactly what he did, which was a terribly brave thing to do … but the show must go on! Even though he commented on the loss of his child in the newspapers at the time, he didn't speak publicly until a while later. He also mentioned it in his book "A Better Me", which came out in 2018.

Of course, it was such a personal and tragic loss, which Jas and I knew only too well, but for someone in the public eye it must have been ten times worse. People can be very cruel and not always as empathetic as we'd like. We'd certainly experienced that.

It's a strange world we live in, where we're not allowed to show our own emotions in the case of a bereavement, especially when it's the death of a child. Just because it's awkward for other people to deal with our grief, we shouldn't be ashamed to express our emotions. It's not good for our mental health if we hold our sorrow inside, just for the sake of others. It feels like we can only really talk about baby loss with people who have also lost a baby.

Thankfully, when I did later join an online bereavement support group, SANDS (Stillbirth and Neonatal Death support), I could share my feelings without any kind of shame or judgement. I didn't feel like an alien with these wonderful people who were suffering with the same heartbreak, no matter how long ago their babies had died.

They had all experienced exactly the same treatment from certain people who were uncomfortable talking to the bereaved parents about the death of their child. Members of the group also agreed that it was far more preferable for people to say: “Are you okay?” or “Can I do anything for you?” instead of crossing the street to avoid speaking about your loss.

It was now time for my six-week check-up with the midwife at the doctor’s surgery. I walked in and she had a big smile on her face. She said she was surprised I’d not brought the baby with me. I stopped in my tracks. I couldn’t believe they had still not updated my records to say that I had a stillborn. I had to tell her. Her smile quickly faded away and she said how sorry she was and that she would update the records immediately. She examined me and said that I’d healed perfectly fine and that she was sorry again for not knowing about my loss. I told her that it wasn’t her fault. As I walked outside, I bumped into someone that both Jas and I knew, although she was more of an acquaintance really. She asked me how I was doing and gave me a hug. I said I was as well as I could be, and she replied in a chirpy voice, 'You don't need to worry, you're still young and can have another one.' I looked at her in disbelief! I felt like saying, "What did you just say?!! I can have another one. Don't worry!" I was fuming and had to get away from her as quickly as I could, before I blew up. How dare she say that to me! It was shocking how thoughtless some people could be. When Jas arrived home from work, I told him what had happened, and he was angry too. He took my hand. "As hard as it is, we're just going to have to control our feelings around people who make insensitive comments, which has become clear already." I told him I wanted to scream at her actually and say, what if one of your children died? It was just so frustrating that I couldn't bring myself to shout back at these people. Obviously If I did, I would cause a scene and what would society think about that? Goodness me! I guess I needed to do the 'terribly British thing': keep a stiff upper lip and bury my emotions.

I often wanted to say to people what I felt like saying to the woman I'd met outside the surgery: "How would you feel if your child died?" However, I've never been one to be so blunt, and would never say those words. If I did, I'm sure people would respond by saying, "How dare you bring my child into it!' But really, I just wanted them to understand what it might feel like If their child had died. I wanted them to just get a glimpse into how I was feeling. I wasn't wishing it upon them; these were just my thoughts.

It's a problem in our society, that we cannot actually say what we want to, even at our darkest times. I believe this is why there are so many people in our world suffering from depression and mental health issues. Sometimes, I just wanted to wear a tee-shirt that was printed with the words: 'My son just died', so people would understand why I was not a happy, bubbly person, and why I looked at them blankly. Wearing a tee-shirt would have been easier than having to tell people. Although either way is difficult for everyone. Death at any age is not a subject that most people want to talk about, but the death of a child, at any age, is particularly uncomfortable.

So, it occurred to me that bereaved parents needed an understandable title. We are warriors, going through hellish grief whilst our baby angels are in heaven. It's almost as if we have to wear armour to fight the dark that has entered our lives. I was inspired by Archangel Michael when I thought of the title 'Angel Warrior.' No matter what sort of situation you find yourself in, Michael will give you the necessary courage and strength to deal with it. He also provides protection, which is how I see an Angel Warrior - protecting the spirit, soul and memory of the child that was lost.

I have chosen purple as the colour for the cover of this book. It is associated with Archangel Michael and is meant to be the colour of his aura.

Summary

Obviously, life carried on for others, and I'm happy that it did, for their sakes. However, I was still in the depth of grief and in a very dark place. I wouldn't want anyone to feel like this. I wouldn't wish it on my worst enemy.

Unfortunately, pressure comes from other people, and it's fair to say you need to stand your own ground. If you don't want to do something they might suggest, don't do it. No matter how well-meaning people seem to be, go by how you and your partner feel.

What becomes clear over the weeks after losing your child, is that you know the people who are truly there for you. Steven, my brother, had been an immense support for both of us, and it was at this time that Jas said: “He's not just my brother-in-law, he’s my brother.” The difference it made for Jas to have Steven’s support was clear in those words. It's important that the fathers of the deceased child also get as much support as they can from their friends and relatives, especially since they may be finding it hard to be strong for the grieving mother. My husband knew that it was ten times harder for me because I had given birth to Luca; he had grown in my womb and I had a bond with him, way before Jas could feel his kicks. This is important to remember for a father supporting a grieving partner. She has been through so much more physically, emotionally and mentally. Childbirth is exhausting for a woman, and it is a hundred times worse when it’s a stillborn. It’s important though that fathers take care of their own mental health, so that they can be there for the mother of their stillborn child.

You'll start seeing the true colours of people around you in the first few weeks. Shocking things will be said - words that you can never imagine people would ever think, let alone say. Trust me, it's hard to bite your tongue and not shout back at these insensitive people.

As time goes on, I can't say that it gets easier, it just becomes different. You will find your new normal, but it takes time.

However, for those supporting the couple in their bereavement, please do the simple things that will help them. Those first eight to ten weeks are so important. Whilst you still get on with your life, please keep checking in on the couple too.

For other people, please do not treat the couple like lepers. Don't keep your distance, and then turn up in their lives when you think they are 'over it.' Understand that no-one gets over the loss of their child. If you cannot understand the parents' feelings, try closing your eyes and imagining that someone has told you that your child has died. Your heart will hurt immediately just by trying to imagine it, and your eyes will fill with tears. You won't want to imagine the worse thing ever happening to you. But remember this is this couple's new reality.

The couple will be a new version of themselves,

so don't look for who they used to be. They are now living a new normal and finding their feet slowly. They're having to walk again with a missing part of their heart - the part that died with their baby.

Chapter Three

The Final Goodbye

I was going deeper and deeper into an extremely dark place. The pain, the emptiness, the sheer horror, tugging at my heart. I needed to be with my boy. I still had my post pregnancy body and no baby to show for it. The excruciating pain of the emptiness was killing me, and during this dark time I could not think of anything else apart from being with Luca. There was only one obvious way that I could be with my baby, and that was to take my own life. So, I began to think of the easiest, quickest and most pain-free way to do it. I wasn't thinking of anything else. I needed a way out of my misery, and I wanted to be with Luca again. I didn't feel I could go on living without him.

I looked at the wall clock and suddenly realised that soon Jas would be home from work. Oh my gosh, Jas! He would be the one to find my body! What was I thinking? I couldn't do that to him. He was already grieving, and then to come home and find that I'd killed myself. It was just too awful to imagine the pain it would cause him, and it stopped me in my tracks. I'd been so hellbent on taking my own life, but I hadn't even thought of what it would do to my husband, as well as the rest of my family. It wasn't until I looked at the time that I even gave Jas any consideration. Thankfully I did though, and it was the thought of my lovely husband finding me that stopped me from taking my own life. I put my head in my hands and sobbed my heart out, knowing what I had intended to do.

From what I've learned, it seems that when people do contemplate suicide, they're only focused on ending their emotional pain, and in a way they're not really in their right mind – the pain has taken over. I was being totally selfish in my needs and feelings. My strongest desire was to be with Luca and I hadn't thought of anyone else.

I feel so fortunate that I did think of Jas, or perhaps God, or Luca, had a hand in it. My advice to anyone contemplating suicide would be to please consider the person who finds your body, and the devastating effect your death will have on all your loved ones.

When Jas arrived home, he could see that I had been crying a lot, as my eyes were puffy and red. “What’s the matter?” he asked. I told him that I’d thought about taking my own life, because I couldn’t stand the pain and the emptiness of not having Luca. I told him that I couldn’t go through with it though, because I thought of him finding my body, and I knew I couldn’t do that to him. Jas held me so close asking me to promise that I would never ever do anything like that. He told me that he couldn’t live without me; that I was his life now. “Promise me, please, that you won’t ever think of doing that again.” I cried and told him that I loved him too much, and that I would never do it. That evening, Jas messaged his manager at work to say that I was in a bad way, and that he needed to work from home for a few days. His manager agreed, and I knew deep inside, Jas was making sure he was with me just in case I had suicidal thoughts again.

I knew I needed help, and Jas agreed. This was actually the first time I had contacted SANDS (Stillbirth and Neonatal Death Support). I wasn't ready to talk to people face to face, so I went online and typed in my first message to SANDS. I said that just a few weeks ago I’d lost my son who was stillborn at 36 weeks, and I was struggling. I wrote that I felt so empty, useless, and guilty and felt like my body had failed my son. I got lots of responses, from ladies who had similar experiences. Some asked if there had been a post-mortem, and if we'd had the results yet. I told them we hadn't, but I did know that there had been nothing wrong with the placenta and that the pediatrician had said that everything was fine with Luca. One lady came back and said that the post-mortem would give me the answers and that I should hang in there. I knew that's what I had to do, hang in there, and that there was nothing else I could do. That week we also went to pick up Luca's ashes. To my horror his ashes were in a simple small square cardboard box. I told the funeral home that I wouldn't take them like that, and that our son's ashes should be in an appropriate container. They showed us a variety of containers that were available, and we chose a tube with a picture of a teddy bear on it.

The following week we received a letter to say that the post-mortem results were in, and that we had an appointment to go and speak to an obstetrician at the hospital on the 22nd of August.

We had decided to scatter Luca's ashes in a river

in Leicestershire, and strangely enough we had planned it for the afternoon of 22nd August. In Indian tradition, scattering the ashes in water means that you are setting the soul of the departed free. I'd never known anything else, so I didn't question that decision. But I've regretted it ever since.

In the morning of the 22nd, as we drove to our appointment with the obstetrician, I kept going over what they might tell me: that it was my fault, or maybe there was something in his genetics that caused Luca's death and that we could not have known about or prevented. I guess in my head I was thinking that one of these reasons might give me some closure, and that this might help me move forward in some way. I suppose I really wanted to hear that there was nothing that could have been done, and that even if he had lived, he would not have survived. That was the only kind of closure I could think of which would give me some relief from the endless pain and guilt that I was feeling.

The obstetrician asked us how we were. Obviously, we weren't in a good place, but said that Jas was back at work and that I was still struggling and feeling a lot of emptiness. She began asking me how I'd felt during my pregnancy. I told her it had been great; that I had barely any morning sickness and that it was a textbook pregnancy. There was nothing that I could pinpoint that I could have done wrong. She looked at me and told me I hadn't done anything wrong. She mentioned that I'd had the diabetes check, which was all fine and that all my other checks were satisfactory. Jas mentioned that we had been to the hospital a week before for what we thought was leaking water, and the obstetrician said she'd seen the notes about that and where they'd marked down that everything was okay. I asked if something had been missed. She looked through the charts and then became concerned and encircled a chart from the day we had our growth scan at 24 weeks. She asked if anybody had followed up on this, and I said 'no,' and asked her what she meant. Why did it need to be followed up? She said the chart showed that Luca was small for his gestation period. I said I didn't understand as we had been told that everything was fine. She pointed to the chart and showed us the line that indicated he was on the smaller side for his abdominal measurement and told us that this was something that would normally have needed a follow up. She explained, however, that the post-mortem did not find anything wrong with Luca. He was perfectly formed. The only thing they could put his death down to was an IUGR, which stands for Intrauterine Growth Restriction. She said if this had been picked up, then they could have monitored it. When I heard those words right there, it made me wonder, does that mean my son should be here? That just took my breath away. I couldn't comprehend the words that were coming out of her mouth. After that, the conversation became a blur, I couldn't focus on anything else apart from her saying that there should have been a follow-up.

Back at home, Jas and I were just so confused. We had been told everything was fine, how could they miss that Luca was small? It seemed like a very significant thing that had been missed. The person in charge of the sonograph had been so busy talking about the man who lived in our house before us, that perhaps she didn't do her job correctly that day. She was so consumed with talking about other things, which were completely irrelevant. It didn’t escape me that it had been Friday the 13th of April. I will always remember it as the day that my son’s growth scan was incorrectly read. I will always hate Friday the 13th from now on. I asked Jas if that meant Luca should be here. He replied that he didn't know and that although the doctor hadn't really said that in as many words, reading between the lines, perhaps 'yes'.

"So, were they negligent?" I shouted.

Jas explained that we couldn't know that for sure, but based on what she'd told us and the fact that it wasn't followed up on, it sounded like it could be negligence. I thought about the possibility, that my baby wasn't here because some woman hadn't done her job correctly and instead kept talking about stupid stuff, which might have cost us our son's life, and I screamed in frustration. Jas held me. He was obviously as frustrated as me and was also trying to take it all in himself.

So, I didn't get the closure that I'd been hoping for. Instead, my head was spinning with the thought of someone having missed a very vital part of my son's growth chart and that there was a chance that he could have survived. This was the opposite of what I thought I'd be coming out of that meeting with. I don't think there are any words that can actually really explain what was going through my head at that time. What I wanted to do was find that woman and show her the chart and scream at her that it was because of her that my son wasn't here. I was processing this information, and I'd have to replay it over and over again in my head to really understand what had been said. I needed to discuss with Jas if there was any action we could take, but this was no time for a hasty decision.

We decided to go ahead and do what we'd said we were going to do that day, set our baby free. For the rest of the day, we focused on that. It was beautiful and sunny as we made our way to Leicestershire with Luca's ashes in the little teddy bear tube. I'd also taken some flowers from the garden to scatter with Luca's ashes in the water, so that he had something from home.

We arrived at the front office, which was a part of a cafe really, overlooking the river, and explained we had booked to scatter ashes on the river that day. Which, incidentally, would cost one hundred pounds. Initially, the gentleman seemed shocked to see us, but then said that he knew I was Sharon. "And this is my husband, Jas", I said. The man took us towards the boat that we were going to be using and introduced us to the driver who explained that he'd take us to a quiet part of the river. We said, 'thank you', and got onto the boat. As it moved along, we looked at the scenery around us. It was very peaceful. There were other people on their boats, some summer paddle boats and others just enjoying the sunny weather. We stopped at a spot which was very quiet, and the driver told us we could have as much time as we needed. We held the teddy tube containing Luca's ashes. It was now time to say a final goodbye to our little boy. Both Jas and I began to cry as, with shaking hands, we held the tube with its cute teddy bear design containing Luca's ashes, and removed the lid.

I said, "This is the final part, beloved son. We won't get to hold you again after this, until we meet again in heaven. Please float away, be free, and rest in peace. We will love you and miss you with every beat of our hearts for the rest of our lives. You will always be our very special first-born."

Jas began slowly releasing Luca's ashes into the water whilst I sprinkled the flowers I'd brought from home to go with our son on his final journey.

We sobbed so much as we did it, whispering about loving Luca. When the tube was empty, we watched as the ashes started floating away with the flowers. I love the summer, and especially the sunshine, which helped make that day right - the water was shining from the sun rays above as if God was shining down on us as we said our final goodbye to the soul of our souls who we would never know. After a short while, I gestured to the driver that we were ready to go back. He turned the boat around and off we went. I looked back and saw the flowers floating away. We sat for a while back at the café, had an ice cream and looked at the river; then we went to pay the owner of the boat. He wouldn't take our money. It was then I understood why he had looked shocked earlier. It was because he had noticed the teddy bear tube and realised that the ashes were of a child. We insisted on paying him something, but he wouldn't take our money. He wished us well on our journey, shook Jas's hand and gave me a pat on the shoulder, as if to say, 'I feel for you.' It was a lovely gesture, and we thanked him.

On the way home we spoke about how perfect the day was in terms of weather and being able to do this for Luca, but in the back of our minds we were still thinking about what we'd heard at the hospital meeting that day. We couldn't get that out of our heads, but I think we were both just too exhausted by then to talk about it any-more.

A week or so later there was an article in - I think it was the Daily Mail - about a couple who had been through a similar stillborn experience in a hospital down south. They had been taking legal action and it was found that negligence was in-volved and was the reason their child was still-born. Jas sent me a link to the article saying that it seemed like a similar story to ours. The article had the name of the solicitors the couple had used, so I suggested to Jas that we call them lat-er when he was home. We discussed it after din-ner and decided that I should call the solicitors and explain what had happened with us. “We owe it to Luca,” Jas said.

The following day I called the solicitors and spoke to the lady who had dealt with the case reported in the newspaper. She asked me ques-tions and decided that our experience was very similar to that case. Consequently, she agreed to take our case on a ‘no win, no fee’ basis since we didn't have the money to take it to court ourselves. She then asked for all the hospital details, so that she could request medical records of my pregnancy. We knew this was the start of the legal case, but what we didn't know then, was how long it would take before we could get an answer.

Summary

Although it hardly needs stating, as sad and bereft as you may be, taking one's own life is never the answer. This won't bring your child back and it will leave your loved ones with more sorrow and despair than you could ever imagine. Suicide is a desperate act and might be considered somewhat selfish, but in my case, the need to be with Luca was foremost in my mind. It is often said that people who take their own lives are not in their right minds. I can understand this. They're certainly in what they think is their right mind – they've made a decision which they think will make them happy and take away the pain. For me, even though it might have seemed to be the only way I could be reunited with my baby, how could I possibly know if that's what would have happened. How can anyone know? I do believe that God has a plan for us all, and as heart-breaking as it was to lose my child, eventually I had to come to terms with it. This experience has made me stronger, given me a reason to live, and hopefully to make a difference in the lives of others.

I can't stress enough the importance of asking questions during your pregnancy and making sure if there's any hint of a potential problem, that you're on top of the situation. Luca's growth scan hadn't been read correctly because the nurse was distracted with chit-chat unrelated to the scan. She might have been good at her job, but I wasn't her main concern on that dreaded Friday the 13th, nor was my baby. This was negligence as far as Jas and I were concerned, but in the end there was nothing we could do about it, except be more vigilant in the future.

Reflecting at this stage, it's clear to see that when you think you're doing everything right, you are often not thinking straight enough to understand all the consequences of certain actions. Only then do you realise that you would have probably done things in a different way. If only we all had such hindsight at every stage of our lives!

For example, when I said that I would later regret scattering Luca's ashes, it was because I found out that you can actually have jewellery made out of ashes. If I had known that, I would have had Luca's ashes made into something I could wear, so that he would be with me every day. Alternatively, there are also glass ornaments that can be made with the ashes inside - something beautiful to keep in the home. Although I didn't think this was possible, my friend Alison Fleming of Harmony Glass, was able to retrieve remnants of Luca's ashes left in the teddy bear tube and put them inside a beautiful glass angel. There is a light underneath the angel and at night the angel glows and the ashes sparkle almost as if Luca is alive. Alison gave this angel to me as a gift, and I really appreciate her kindness and thoughtfulness. It means such a lot.

Chapter Four

New Beginnings

Now that we knew there was nothing wrong with Luca, we were given the all-clear to start trying for another baby if we so wished. Jas and I had discussed whether we wanted to do this right away or give it some time. I knew that I was a mum without her baby, and my arms were aching with the emptiness of not being able to hold my child, and to be the mother I was meant to be. I also knew that having another child would not replace Luca, but that it would help to fill the absolute horrific void in my life.

In order for me to be able to have another child, I needed to be ovulating. My menstrual cycle had not come back at all since giving birth to Luca. It would be fair to say that the grief, the stress, and everything else that goes with having lost a child, played a significant part in this.

At this point I was using the SANDS online support site quite a lot. I'd spoken to bereaved mothers and asked them for their thoughts on when would be the right time to try and have another baby. Clearly everyone is different and that is exactly the response I got. They were all very empathetic, of course, but it was clearly a decision that had to be right for me and Jas. One woman said, “There will never be a right time, and the longer you wait, the more anxious you might get about it. If you do it straight away, you’ll still be anxious about it.”

Let's face it, a subsequent pregnancy was not going to be easy and would be filled with anxiety, no matter how long or not we left it. We were both parents without their child and wanted nothing more than to be parents. We gave it a lot of thought and came to the same conclusion. We decided that once my menstrual cycle returned, we would start trying for a baby.

A couple of weeks earlier, my aunt and sister had asked me to join them to go to a theme park with my sister’s children. I realised it was also another attempt to get me out of the house. I took them up on the offer and Jas told me he thought it might be good for me to go out with the children because they always made me laugh. At the theme park I noticed so many mothers with pushchairs and small babies and had to try my hardest all day not to cry; I didn't want to ruin the day out for the children. But it did make it even more clear to me just how much I really did need to have another baby.

Meanwhile, my mum said it would be good for us to get away and have a change of scenery - a place where no one knew about our loss. She suggested we could perhaps go for a city break in Europe. She offered to pay for it and told us not to worry about the finances. We decided to go to Rome since we'd always wanted to go there. Making all the arrangements gave me something to do, and I had something to look forward to as well. So, In the second week of September, we headed off to Rome.

We arrived in Rome not too late in the evening, but it was dark, as our bus had been delayed on arrival. We checked into our hotel, got into the room, put our cases in and headed straight out for something to eat as we were starving. We were staying near the centre and there were lots of restaurants and bars nearby. We were drawn to an Irish bar where cheerful music was playing. It was a really warm evening, so we sat outside and watched the locals going by. The atmosphere on the street was great, so we knew we'd chosen the right place. We had a nice simple dinner - burger and chips, if I remember correctly. Not exactly very Italian!

The next morning, after a good sleep, we had breakfast and then went off for some sightseeing.

We had a map, so we knew where to go and, fortunately, all the sites were easy to walk to. The only exception was Vatican City, which was too far for us to walk to, but we'd figured out a way to get there on the Metro underground.

There was so much to see, but don't ask me to recall the names of everywhere we went, as I really can't remember. What I did notice, massively, was that wherever we went and whichever street we turned down, I would see Luca's name. I suppose I'd forgotten that Luca was the Italian name for Luke, and I certainly had no idea just how popular it was in Italy. Maybe it was just a coincidence, but I saw Luca everywhere! It was quite comforting and made me feel as if he was on the trip with us.

It also seemed that in some way, Luca had led us

to Italy to show us that he was always with us, no matter where in the world we were. It really gave me such a sense of peace and calm.

We went to the Spanish Steps and looked at the stunning views. Then on our way to the Trevi Fountain, we walked through a quiet square where there was a bistro and small shop. I was just astonished when I looked up at the name of the square and saw that it was 'Saint Luca Square!' I took a photo and smiled. It was just another sign that Luca was with us. It really made me feel good. Jas put his arm around me as if to say, 'Yeah, that's our boy.'

It was very busy at the Trevi Fountain with so many people taking photos, trying to get the best shot. It was such an idyllic place though, so I found a spot to sit down, and Jas took my photo. They say that if you throw a coin in the fountain and make a wish, it comes true. Well, just try and guess what I was wishing for? Yep, I was wishing for my menstrual cycle to come back so that we could try for a baby again. Never in a million years would I ever have thought I would be wishing to have my period, but, oh yes, that was what I needed now, so that I could ovulate. I wanted to be pregnant, and I wanted a baby.

We were in Rome for three nights and enjoyed every minute of it. It was almost like a second honeymoon for Jas and me. We had been to most of the main attractions, including the Colosseum and decided to visit Vatican City on our last day in Rome.

We headed out early because we knew the Vatican would get full very quickly. We took the Metro, which was quite easy, and as we walked towards the Vatican, we thought how amazing it was. As a Christian, the Vatican was definitely one place I had always wanted to visit, as well as Bethlehem and Jerusalem, and finally here I was in Rome in one of the holiest of places. I was so excited.

There were quite a few people selling audio tours, which we thought would be a good idea – not only because we'd learn so much about the history of Vatican City, but we'd also heard that we would get to queue-jump if we were part of an audio tour. So we did exactly that. As we were jumping the queues, I looked at Jas and laughed; we'd definitely done the right thing. The group wasn't very big - I think there were only about ten of us - but once we got inside the Vatican it was very busy.

I was just amazed at what I saw, as well as heard on the audio. It was just magical. Before we entered the magnificent Sistine Chapel, I went into a little shop selling memorabilia. I saw some beautiful prayer beads that looked like pearl and silver entwined, and I purchased these, along with a few other souvenirs.

I felt so at ease in the Vatican and experienced an overwhelming sense of inner peace. It was the type of feeling I normally only got at Coventry Cathedral. Although there were lots of people around me, they didn't block any of the peace I was feeling inside. I sat down in one of the corners, which was quieter and away from lots of the loud people taking lots of photos. I say loud, but they were just tourists talking to each other, trying to be heard amongst the mass of people there. Tucked away in this nice little corner, I prayed that we would welcome a child the following year, before Luca's anniversary, and that the child would be completely healthy, and that I would be too.

We arrived home early afternoon the next day,

and it was nice to get back - the sun was shining to welcome us as well. Jas still had another day off work, and we just chilled out at home, watching TV and eating a takeaway.

About ten days later, guess what? My menstrual cycle appeared! I was delighted, as was Jas. At this time though I wasn't going to put all my hopes into conceiving straight away as it had taken us four months with Luca. I was also studying for my Prince 2 certificate, which was required for me to qualify in project management. It was good that I had some focus. It was what I needed at this time, so that I didn't go insane with the thought of trying to conceive. A few weeks later, I was in a classroom surrounded by people all studying for their Prince 2 qualification. It was a crash course over four and a half days. I was surprised to see that my sister-in-law's aunt was on the same course. It was a nice surprise and I was happy to see someone there that I knew. I hadn't seen her since Luca had died, so our initial conversation in our first break was about Luca. We stood to one side of the room because obviously there were going to be tears.

I worked hard that week and really applied myself. I wanted to pass and finally have my certificate as a project manager. This was the same week that I also ovulated. However, and strangely, it was on the day that I didn't have homework. I laugh about it now as it was definitely important at that time. I had passed the first part of the project management course, the Foundation, and then I had to sit the exam for Practitioner on the following Friday morning. It was quite intense, but I got through it, and my course was finished. I wouldn't get the results for two weeks but that was fine. I had finished the course and had given it my all. Since I'd passed the Foundation part of the course, if I passed the Practitioner level too, then I had done a bloody good job! As a grieving mum trying to study whilst thinking about conceiving, and everything else that was going on in my head, I thought it would be a miracle if I actually passed the Practitioner level.

The following week I just chilled and didn't really do a lot. I think I was mentally exhausted from all the time and energy I had put into the course. I knew that the coming weekend would mark ten days from the day I had ovulated, and I could take a pregnancy test. Yes, that's right, I'm one of those people–who start to count from the day of ovulation, and I knew ten days was the earliest I could take a pregnancy test. I'd done it with Luca, and I was going to do it the same way now.

That Sunday morning it'd been a whole week of waiting, and I woke up and took the test. I didn't tell Jas what I was doing though. It was enough pressure for me, and I didn't want to put it on him as well. I brushed my teeth, and had a wash whilst waiting for the test results to appear on the screen. I dried myself off and I went over to have a look. Wow! I was pregnant, and this was the first time we'd tried! I was pregnant!! I was giddy with excitement but crying at the same time knowing that there was going to be a long journey ahead of us.

I picked up the test and went downstairs. Jas was watching cricket. I sat next to him and handed him the test. He looked at me and his eyes immediately filled up with tears. We just held each other and cried happy tears. I suggested that we wait before telling anyone, and I would call the midwife the next day and make an appointment. We knew that this time around things were going to be really hard, but we knew what to look out for too. We were also determined that no one, and I mean no one, was going to brush us off with saying ‘everything’s fine’, because this time I would want everything explained thoroughly.

• • • • • • • • • • • •

Jas had already decided he was going to watch football with some friends at the pub that afternoon. I can't remember who was playing, but it must have been Manchester United because that's the only time he would ever go out or watch football with his friends. A lot of them were United fans, and they liked to get together for those matches.

He’d popped in to see his folks on the way there and they'd been talking to him about building a shed at the back of our garden. Now I mean, not an ordinary shed, but a brick built shed, an outhouse really. Jas being a sort of ‘yeah, yeah’ type of guy - he doesn't really listen or take in what's actually being said sometimes - his parents took this as an agreement. They wanted to pay for it, which was obviously very generous of them, and Jas probably thought he couldn’t really say “no”.

This shed was to be built by someone we knew, who was just starting out as a builder, and had a few people working for him. With Jas's 'yeah, yeah' type of approach, the next thing I knew was the builder and Jas's dad were at our house measuring the back of the garden to see how big the shed could be. I was a bit surprised and taken aback by what was going on and asked what they were doing since, in my opinion, we didn't even need a shed. We had nothing to put in it. However, they said that it was already agreed, and it was as if my opinion didn't count for anything, even though it was my house too, for goodness' sake! Jas's dad said that we'd soon start using it, just as they did with their shed – it was like an extra kitchen for Jas's mum where she made her curries.

I told Jas's dad that I wasn't the type of person who made big pots of curry in a shed and would much prefer to cook in my kitchen. He laughed. I most certainly didn't need a shed taking over the whole of my garden. It makes me laugh now thinking back on it. I wasn't completely against the idea, and wouldn't have minded a small shed, but I was just surprised at how quickly they came to measure it up.

I called Jas and asked him if he knew what had just happened. He laughed and said he hadn't actually agreed to it, he'd just said 'yeah, yeah, maybe'. "Well, your 'yeah, yeah', as usual, has now been taken as a full on 'yes'," I told him. Oh, I was so annoyed at him that he'd not told them to just leave it for now and wait until he'd discussed it with me.

I suppose, in his defence, he was thinking about the fact that we'd had a positive pregnancy test that morning, and anything else that anyone was saying to him was just going in one ear and out the other. I was thinking: Well, I've had a positive pregnancy test this morning, and now I want to take things easy and let things glide along with no stress or pressure. Little did I know that that thought was about to be challenged.

The next morning, the builder and his team of three people knocked on the door and told me they had arrived to build our shed/outbuilding. I was just gob-smacked! "Are you seriously starting this right now?" I couldn't believe it. What a way to start my new pregnancy. Obviously, my hormones were playing a big part in my reaction here. I just didn't need this right now; I needed to relax and take it easy. I was mad at Jas, not them - obviously they didn't know I was pregnant. I wanted Jas to have the guts to tell them to leave it, as we didn't want it because we had other things to think about, but it was too late, they were already starting to prepare the foundation. It took about three weeks to build, during which time I'd had an appointment with the midwife, and she was delighted to hear that I was pregnant again. She explained how I would be carefully monitored and that she would immediately write to the hospital and assign an obstetrician. In these three weeks, instead of resting as I had wanted to, I was constantly making tea for the builders. I was having to put up with dirt and noise, and waking up early, to let people in and out of my house to use the facilities. It was not the best start to my pregnancy and let's not forget, I was still grieving as well. Just because I had a positive pregnancy test, did not mean that I had suddenly stopped grieving for Luca, and nor would I ever.

The following week I got a letter saying that I had passed my Prince 2 Practitioner Exam. I was delighted. I hadn't really expected to pass, considering everything that was still going on.

This was good news, because it meant I could get a job in so many businesses, including IT, HR, finance and retail. I called Jas at work and told him immediately. He was very happy for me as he knew I'd put so much work into these studies, and at such a difficult time of our lives too.

A week later it was Diwali, the festival of lights for many Indian religions. This was something I hadn't really celebrated massively in the past, as I am Christian, and Jas doesn't really pay too much attention to it either. Nevertheless, I would always leave a light on at night as my aunt had told me too many years ago. Regardless of whether we did or not, we were still in a very dark place grieving for our son, and had no desire to celebrate anything, not even Christmas.

I received a message from a woman we knew asking what we were doing for Diwali celebrations. This came as a surprise as she had never in the previous years ever asked this. I explained we had no desire to be celebrating anything at this time as we were still grieving for our son. I was very polite and clear. She responded extremely abruptly and told me to 'get over it', and 'get a grip'. She also added: 'It's not our fault that your son died'.

I was shocked and disgusted to my core at her words. I was crying by the time Jas came home. He asked me what was wrong, and I showed him my phone and the messages I'd received. He was livid and couldn't believe that anyone would even think these words, let alone say them or type them with such clarity and malice. It was so insensitive, and it felt as if she was trying to hurt me even more than I was already hurting. I can't quite remember what happened at this point, but I think Jas sent a text to this woman, from my phone, telling her to leave me alone. Then he texted her husband telling him to ask his wife to stop texting me as she was upsetting me deeply. It was certainly one or the other, or both. This bugged Jas for so many days afterwards, and on the weekend, he took my phone to show someone he was close to the messages and asked if we were overreacting. This person was shocked that anyone could even send such hurtful messages, especially as this woman had children of her own.

Both Jas and I often heard this particular couple

saying offensive things after Luca had died. The husband actually told Jas that he was being too sensitive because he wouldn't attend a party given by a mutual friend. This time it caused a huge argument, and from then on it was the end of our relationship with this man and woman.

That aside, we had managed to get an appointment with the obstetrician who had given us the post-mortem results. She was delighted that I was pregnant and assured me that I would be treated as 'high risk' and would be well taken care of. She also said that she would want to see me on a regular basis. At present though, she wanted to have a little look inside and make sure there was a heartbeat. As I was literally in the early weeks of pregnancy this was an internal examination as opposed to an external scan. After seeing the little heartbeat on the screen and receiving confirmation that 'yes', there was a little baby growing inside of me, the obstetrician told us that when the baby was twelve weeks, she would put me on aspirin. This was just to make sure that my blood stayed thin enough to feed my baby throughout my pregnancy and was obviously the first stage of eliminating anything that might cause me to lose the baby. I had a scan at ten weeks, and everything was good, and then we had our official twelve-week scan after that. Needless to say, we were in and out of the hospital maternity unit for the entire pregnancy. There were many appointments with long waiting times, but all I could think about was: will my baby be alive at the end of this?

We still hadn't told anyone that we were pregnant, even after the twelve-week scan. We just wanted to go as long as we could without having to mention it.

It was Christmas and New Year just before the twelve-week scan, but I didn't even put the Christmas tree up. It wasn't the Christmas that I had planned it to be, and I just didn't have any joyous feelings at all. There were no little baby gifts with Luca's name on under the tree or in a stocking. I couldn't bring myself to celebrate, and all I wanted was to hibernate and not see anyone. My mum insisted that it would do us good to be with the family, and she knew that none of us were really going to enjoy this Christmas as much as we should have. She thought it would be nice if we at least had Christmas dinner together, and Jas and I agreed to that.

I had bought Jas an Everton shirt, which I had already planned before Luca had died. It was going to be his gift to his dad on his first Christmas. The Everton shirt had Luca's name and birth date written on the back. I still did it and on the gift card I wrote, 'To my daddy. Even though I'm not here with you, this present is something Mummy had already thought of before I died. I still want you to have it because I still live on in your heart.' Jas cried when he saw it and read the message. It was just something I needed to do to remember Luca at Christmas, just for us two.

Jas went to his parents to give a few gifts to his family, but I didn't go. I really wasn't up to it. His mum called me and asked why I hadn't come, and I just burst out crying on the phone, telling her that it wasn't a joyous day for me. I also knew that I would have to pretend to be happy, and I just couldn't face it.

I realised that at times I behaved quite differently with certain people. For some I had to pretend to be okay, just to make them feel comfortable, and for others, I could actually show my true feelings. I had agreed to go to my family because I knew I wouldn't have to pretend or hide how I was feeling.

On Christmas Day, when we arrived at my parents' home in Leicestershire, I burst into tears as soon as my mum opened the door. She was also crying, and we went into one of the small rooms where my brother Steven was, and we all cried together. Then I went into the kitchen where my sister-in-law, Olivia, was peeling vegetables and she gave me a hug.

It was definitely a day of ups and downs. My dad made a speech just before dinner thanking the Lord for this special day. He also mentioned the people who were missing: Sunny because he was working abroad, and Luca who was in heaven. This again made me cry, so I left the table and had another good cry before I returned. Olivia's parents and sisters joined us for the day, and it sort of broke things up a little because it added a different atmosphere, and the conversation was varied and interesting.

The New Year went by in a blur. I honestly can't remember what we did. I think we were in bed early. I was still feeling quite tired with it being my first trimester.

Time was dragging, as I wanted my pregnancy to fast forward. I still had my post-pregnancy body which was obviously disguising some of the pregnancy in the early stages. We knew there would be a point at which we wouldn’t be able to disguise it as a post-pregnancy body any longer and would have to tell people that I was pregnant. Luckily, we managed to get to about sixteen or seventeen weeks before we started telling people. We told immediate family only and our very closest friends, who I think of as family anyway.

It was now early February 2013, and my mum and Dad were being baptised at Coventry Cathedral where they had completed their Alpha course. I wore one of Jas's hoodies to disguise the fact I was pregnant. There was a nice little celebration afterwards in Saint Michael’s house next to the cathedral. Food was served and everyone talked merrily. I could tell people were looking at me, but they certainly weren't saying anything, and I’m sure it never occurred to them that I might be pregnant. It just felt it was a bit too soon to be telling the wider group and I didn't want to say anything on that day because it was about my mum and Dad's baptisms.

Within the next couple of weeks, we did start

telling family and friends. We weren't deliberately calling everyone telling them excitingly that we were pregnant again - that feeling really wasn't there. The innocence and enjoyment of having a normal pregnancy had been taken away from us. We had gone through this before, and at the end, our baby had died. So, this time it was a case of confirming that I was pregnant and hoping for the best.

When people congratulated us, I felt like telling them to save their congratulations until the baby was here safe and sound. Obviously, it's a natural instinct for people to say 'congratulations', but since Luca had died, if ever I've heard of a pregnancy, I've always said, "That's great news," and I've saved the congratulations until the baby has arrived safely and mother and baby are both well. To my delight, whilst calling a few of my cousins to tell them I was pregnant, I found out that my cousin, Karen, was also pregnant, and she was two months behind me, with her baby due in September. This was lovely because we agreed that in a few months we would do some shopping together. We did do that, and it was really nice that we were pregnant at the same time, because it felt good to have someone else to talk to about the pregnancy. It was also good knowing that our babies were going to be close in age, and as Karen and I were close cousins, we hoped that our children would be close too. When Jas told his family, they were so happy, and his sister gave him a big hug.

I bought a Doppler monitor so that I could check on the baby's heartbeat at home myself. I knew there could be times when the monitor might not work straight away, but I wasn't going to let that get to me. Both Jas and I needed peace of mind, and the monitor was at least something that, we hoped, would help give us that. Jas also worked one or two days from home to keep an eye on me. He was a sweetheart. Still is!

It had taken longer for me to feel the kicks this time because my body wasn't as slim, or so I was told. I didn't actually start feeling the kicks until I was about nineteen weeks pregnant, although with Luca it had been much sooner. We knew by now that we were having a boy, and when the obstetrician gave us the news, Jas and I cried. It felt like déjà vu. Also, this baby boy had a due date that was six days before Luca's. You can imagine how even more anxious that made me, especially as it was so similar to my pregnancy with Luca. it all felt so familiar. I had not had much morning sickness and knowing that the due dates were only six days apart just blew my mind. I could see the obstetrician appointment dates coming up, and with just a few days difference, it really did feel like it was Groundhog Day.

Mother's Day came in March. I cried most of the day and stayed in bed longer. Jas made a card on a website with Luca's picture that I keep next to my bed.

It reads: "You will always be my Mummy and I will always be with you." It was signed: "Love you forever, Luca and my little brother Ky."

Just before I was twenty-three weeks pregnant, I was aware that I hadn't felt the baby kick in a while, so I started to do what I did with Luca to get him moving: I had a cold drink, ate something sweet and had a fizzy drink. Jas suggested we use the Doppler monitor on which we'd managed to hear the heartbeat plenty of times. He thought the baby might just be sleeping, and we could reassure ourselves. We got out the Doppler monitor and moved it around, then held it still, then moved it around a bit more. We held it in place but there was no heartbeat. I was getting a little worked up by now, as you can imagine. Jas kept telling me to try and stay calm, but I knew he was a bit worried too. We gave it a little more time as we knew that the Doppler monitor wasn't always one hundred per cent. However, we had previously always found a heartbeat with the monitor, so not feeling the movements and not hearing the heartbeat was, for us, cause for alarm.

We called the hospital. I told them we needed to come in as we couldn't feel the baby moving, and they agreed. Jas messaged his manager and explained what was happening. He was very understanding and said that we should definitely go to the hospital. On arrival, we handed in our information at the reception desk and sat down to wait. I still hadn't felt the baby move. One of the triage midwives refused to give us a CTG and said that as I was not over twenty-four weeks it was not the normal procedure. I explained that our son had been stillborn the year before and that we needed reassurance that our baby was okay. She was still very dismissive and not at all understanding. She said she would speak to someone else and come back to us.

Whilst we were waiting, our bereavement midwife walked past, and she saw that we were in a bit of a state. She asked what was wrong. We explained that we were having trouble getting seen because we hadn't passed twenty-four weeks, and that I hadn't felt the baby kick since this morning. She immediately went inside and spoke to the triage staff, telling them that we needed some reassurance after what we had already been through. Meanwhile, Jas called our obstetrician's secretary to see if she could help us. He left a message and was waiting for a call back.

The triage midwife we'd seen previously then called us in and wired me up to the CTG scanner. This was to make sure there was movement even though I couldn't feel it, and would give us reassurance that the baby was okay. However, the midwife's manner had really taken me aback and made me quite anxious and nervous. We received a call back from our doctor, whilst I was attached to the CTG monitor. She said we could go up to her office and she'd do a proper scan. This was music to our ears, because that is exactly what we needed to do, to see our healthy son on the screen. That's precisely what happened. We could see him moving and looking perfectly fine. As you can imagine, a whole weight was lifted off my shoulders – Jas's too. We were told that the baby was just at the back of the womb which is why I couldn't feel much movement and why we couldn't pick up his heartbeat on the monitor. Our obstetrician told us that in ten days' time, when I was twenty-four weeks pregnant, she'd do a growth scan. So, we made an appointment to go back in ten days. Funnily enough this date was also our wedding anniversary, but I didn't care, I just wanted to see my baby on that day, and in fact every day after that. I knew seeing him on our wedding anniversary though, would seem extra special.

By the time I was due to go for the scan on my twenty-fourth week of pregnancy, I was feeling my baby move around a bit more regularly, so didn't think there was any reason to be alarmed. Even though I was a lot calmer, when the growth scan showed my beautiful healthy baby kicking away whilst the obstetrician took his measurements, I was very relieved.

As she jotted down the measurements, she looked at Jas and I with a serious expression on her face and told us that the baby was measuring small, and in an almost identical way to Luca. I hadn't thought that this could ever happen again, and I just wasn't ready for this news.

Tears built up in my eyes and the obstetrician knew, having taken us through Luca's post-mortem results, what we would be feeling and thinking at this time. She then told us that we should try to get to thirty-one weeks, and then she would deliver the baby early and put him in the NICU (Neonatal Intensive care unit).

Jas and I were beside ourselves. We couldn't believe the same thing was happening again. I had another feeling of déjà vu and I couldn't hold the tears back. The doctor tried to reassure us by saying that she would put us on weekly monitoring with the Baby Wellbeing Department, and that they would scan me every week. They would also carry out a Doppler test, which is where they check that the blood flow to the baby is actually going through correctly and at a good speed. These were all new things we were learning now during this pregnancy that Jas and I never knew about when I was pregnant with Luca. Well, why would we? We depended on the medical professionals to make sure we had all the right information.

Jas had taken half a day's leave from work, and after the scan he had booked a table at Marco Pierre White restaurant in Birmingham for dinner that evening, to celebrate our anniversary.

After the appointment, I didn't really want to go for the anniversary meal but given that the obstetrician had tried to reassure us, we decided to go. So, I put on my maternity black lace dress and we headed to Birmingham for our meal. Needless to say, during the meal all we talked about were all the possible outcomes and what we should be doing now to prepare to get to thirty-one weeks, which was just five weeks away. In some ways, I felt as if I was in good hands because this time the size issue hadn't been missed and we had a very good chance that everything would go well.

The following day I went to Coventry Cathedral, my special place to pray and find inner peace, and I wrote down a prayer. These were the words that I wrote, which I'll never forget.

"Father in heaven, I pray to you to give me the strength I need to carry on through this pregnancy and for the safe arrival of my little boy. If he needs to come out early, please look after him and please give him all the fighting spirit he needs to survive. If we get past the thirty-one weeks, please can he be born at thirty-six weeks and no later than a week before Luca's birthday, because I can't get through Luca's first birthday and anniversary without knowing that this baby is safe in my arms perfectly healthy and that I am a mother to a living child".

The weeks seemed to go by slowly - this already felt like a ten-year pregnancy to me. I was being checked once a week and then twice a week, then three times a week and then every day in the latter stages. We got past the thirty-one weeks and there had been growth, which was great to see. It was fantastic that the growth scan was going in the right direction. The only thing that wasn't great was that then my obstetrician wanted me to go full term, right up to the forty weeks. I didn't want to do this as I had lost Luca at thirty-six weeks on the first day of my maternity leave, so there was absolutely no way I wanted to go to forty weeks. I thought it would be an absolute nightmare for me to go through an extra four weeks not knowing whether my baby was okay or not, and whether he was going to be born alive.

This started to put me in panic mode, and every night after around thirty-three weeks I would force myself to wake up during the night so that I could wake the baby to make sure he was still alive. It was such a stressful time for me, as I'm sure you'll understand, and even though I knew I wasn't doing what was good for the baby waking him up when he was asleep at night, for my own sanity I needed to know that he was alive. When we told the obstetrician that we wanted him to be born earlier, she was adamant that this was not going to happen. She had been an absolutely fantastic obstetrician, and this was the only time that we came to loggerheads.

My closest friends (they all know who they are) had been a huge support to me throughout this pregnancy – they had been making sure I was getting out whenever I needed to and meeting them for coffee and lunch. But at this point, I was crying on the phone to my friends. I told them that the obstetrician wasn't listening to me. "It's my baby and it should be my choice after what I've been through. I don't know why she can't understand what this is doing to me, mentally". My friends were so supportive and totally understood my concerns.

In the end, I decided to write a letter to the obstetrician explaining my thoughts. I told her that we wanted the baby to be delivered early, and that we would sign any necessary papers to say that we understood the risks we were taking by asking for a premature birth. I was thirty-four weeks pregnant when I wrote this letter and the obstetrician still stood by the fact that she wanted us to go full term. I'd told her in the letter that if she could guarantee one hundred percent that my son would arrive safe, healthy and alive, and that I would be okay too, then we would accept her recommendation. However, if there was no such guarantee then she would need to follow our instructions. I also made it clear that we were the ones that were living with the grief and trauma of losing Luca, and ultimately it was our decision as parents not to put our baby in danger. We also said that we knew and had heard of babies being born much earlier than this gestation, and that they had survived and been perfectly healthy. We ended the letter by saying that if she was still not in agreement with us, that we would like to discuss all the options with the head of the Department of Obstetricians.

This is exactly what happened. The letter went to the head of the Obstetrics Department at our hospital and a meeting was then scheduled. Unfortunately, this was cancelled, but it was rearranged within a couple of days. You can imagine how anxious Jas and I were at this point, and I was a bit of a mess, to be fair, whilst describing why I needed my baby to be delivered early. I couldn't really control myself and the tears were flowing. Jas was trying to do most of the talking for me because I was unable to, but the head of Obstetrics said the letter was very articulate and explained my reasons quite clearly. She could see from my reaction and my physical state that it was not good for me to prolong this pregnancy longer than necessary. She looked at the dates of our conception and said she believed I was not quite thirty-six and that she wouldn’t take me to delivery until I was thirty-seven weeks. I told her I believed the dates she had were wrong as I knew exactly the date I ovulated and conceived. I told her I knew this as it was whilst I was on my Prince 2 course for Project Management. Looking at these dates, she agreed that we were so close to thirty-seven weeks that it would be okay for us to deliver the baby sooner. This was a huge relief to both Jas and me.

There were a number of things that needed to be checked. One was that there was availability to deliver our child on the date of the 14th June. I would need to be in hospital for two days prior to that to have steroid injections to mature the baby's lungs. We also discussed the fact that as I had opted to have a caesarean section, I would also need to see the anaesthetist. An appointment was made for two days later, exactly a week before my baby was due to be born. I thanked the obstetrician so much for respecting our request and helping to put me at ease. We left the appointment extremely relieved knowing that our baby would be with us in nine days.

We started thinking about what we needed to do to prepare for that. First Jas needed to tell his boss that our baby was going to be delivered prematurely, so he would need to start his paternity leave earlier than expected. That was crucial as Jas was a team leader and they would need to put certain things in place for him to have his three weeks off - two week's paternity leave and one week's holiday.

Because Jas was unable to attend the appointment I had with the anaesthetist on the Friday, I asked my brother, Steven, to come with me as he was off work and had moved from London back to our family home whilst he was saving up for his own home. It was a blessing in disguise that he wasn't working at this time because he was a great help to me and Jas.

At this point I was also being checked daily by the Wellbeing Centre at the hospital, so I was going from one appointment to another. It was completely hectic but certainly reassuring as we were at this late stage now. The Wellbeing Centre knew how anxious I was, so they even arranged for me to have CTG scans over that last weekend whilst we were at home. My fingers had swelled up so much that I couldn't get my rings off. They were hurting, but there was nothing I could do about it - there was no way they were coming off unless they were cut off and I definitely wasn't going down that route! I knew that the swelling would be reduced as soon as our little man was delivered.

After Steven took me to the appointment with

the anaesthetist and the Wellbeing Centre, where he found out that we were having a boy, he stayed over with us on the weekend and helped Jas put up the crib and Moses basket. He also assembled the car seat and helped get everything else ready in time for me to go to hospital the following Wednesday. I asked him to keep these arrangements to himself.

That weekend the weather was really warm. We'd had some new garden furniture delivered when we'd had our garden redone. It was now nicely landscaped with slabs and minimum grass. It was low maintenance and just the type of garden we needed and wanted after the mess it had been left in after having that shed built at the back of the garden. I was very pleased with it, because finally it was a garden that we could actually use. We had also had to change some of our fencing panels and Jas decided that weekend he would get rid of the mess because he knew he wasn't going to get a chance to do it again. Steven's girlfriend, Grace, joined us and we sat outside eating our breakfast and enjoying the sun.

The little fellow was very active inside me after

breakfast. He dug in his elbow and it was sticking out so far that you could see the shape of it on my stomach. It looked like something out of the 'Alien' movie. I got Steven to put their hands on my stomach and they were shocked at how sharp the baby's elbow felt. Steven asked if the baby was hurting me, and I told him it was uncomfortable but not really hurting. I explained that it hurts more when he kicks me in the ribs. "Ouch!" Steven said, pulling a face.

Summary

Our holiday in Rome made us realise that we really needed a break. It also set Jas and I on a new path, and Luca was with us all the way. It was a magical time and little did we know that we were creating a new future for ourselves. No matter what we're dealing with in life, the truth is that change is the only constant, and will bring us unexpected delights, if we're open. You might feel guilty about enjoying life without your baby, but our lives do go on, even when we're shrouded in grief.

Despite my grief, I continued studying for a career in project management, which gave me a positive focus. I was delighted that I passed all the exams and then felt ready to return to work. Having a focus and planning something other than getting pregnant is essential for your mental health. It helps you remember who you were before your tragedy.

However, when you do go on to have another pregnancy it is full of anxiety. All of the innocent enjoyment of what you should feel during a pregnancy is taken away, and a pregnancy that is nine months feels like nine plus years. I think for me and many others it would have felt like this whether I had left it two years before trying again, or not. Whenever you decide to have a 'rainbow baby' – a term describing the rainbow after the storm of the tragic loss of a child - it will always be filled with that fear of loss again.

Although people want to say 'congratulations' when they hear that you are pregnant again, it's extremely bittersweet. You almost want to say keep your congratulations until the baby is here safely, but again with the way society is, we can't actually say the things that we really want to. Even though we have been through hell, we have to bite our tongues, so that we don't offend anyone else.

What other people need to learn from this is that they should never say: "Everything will be okay this time", when an Angel Warrior becomes pregnant again. Nothing is okay until the baby is born healthy and nestled safely in the arms of its mother. It is also never appropriate to say: "You will have your baby back now." This baby is not a replacement for the baby the mother has lost - it is not the same baby. This is a completely different child.

As an Angel Warrior you are more than entitled to ask for extra checks and seek reassurance throughout this pregnancy. No one should be denying you this. I also feel this is an area where the NHS needs to adapt more. If a pregnant woman has previously experienced the loss of a child, she should be given extra support and care during her next pregnancy.

Sadly, I was ignored and dealt with very rudely by the midwife who refused to allow checks on Ky before I was twenty-four weeks. I feel a minority of midwives lack empathy for those mothers who have lost a baby and who are full of anxiety during their subsequent pregnancy. If I had not complained to the Head of Midwives at the hospital, about my experience with the insensitive midwife, I probably wouldn't have got the extra special treatment that I did thereafter. It's essential to insist on better care during pregnancy, to guarantee that our babies are healthy and have been safely delivered into the world and into our lives.

Chapter Five

Prayers Answered

My hospital bag had been ready for several weeks following the growth scan in April, so everything was ready to go. I had already been told what I would need prior to the birth, and then Jas would bring the baby's bag on the morning of the C-section. Everything was in place and now we were just waiting for those last two days to go by.

I had a private room at the hospital, and I'd taken a couple of books with me, my iPod, phone and chargers. Jas had also paid for a hospital TV subscription so that I could watch the programmes I enjoyed. That always started with 'GMB', 'Lorraine in the Morning', then 'This Morning', followed by 'Loose Women' and then ITV News. The afternoon would be spent reading or maybe watching a movie, but I was comfortable and relaxed and that was the main thing.

Jas, of course, came during visiting hours although they weren't too strict with him, because they knew how important it was for Jas to be there, especially since I was close to the delivery stage.

Every now and again a nurse came in to monitor my blood and sugar levels because I had gestational diabetes. Steroids were also administered by injection, which was a very uncomfortable procedure, I have to say, but it's what I needed to have done to bring my baby out into this world a bit earlier than usual.

The ladies at the Wellbeing Centre also said that I could still go in for my appointments to have a scan and see my baby. I loved to do this as it gave me the added reassurance now that we were at that latter end, although in some ways it made me nervous. I couldn't stop thinking: We're so close now; I hope nothing goes wrong.

I had managed to get to know quite a few of the midwives quite well and they were very accommodating, which was lovely. I had a visit from the manager of the midwives who I'd spoken to previously after making a complaint about the midwife who had not given me my scan before I was twenty-four weeks. She was so kind. She knew what we were going through and that we were having an early delivery. Everything was on standby just in case baby wasn't too well when he was born, so even the Neonatal Department was ready to take him, if necessary. It was very reassuring to have all this extra help on hand, and when I was alone it gave me time to reflect.

One of my biggest realisations was that my prayers were being answered. I had written in my prayer at Coventry Cathedral that I wanted my baby to be born no later than a week before Luca's birthday, and this was exactly what was happening. Although I was nervous, I still trusted God to deliver my baby perfectly healthy and safe.

On Thursday, my second day in the hospital and after having the steroid injections, I became a little overindulgent at lunchtime, and had apple crumble and custard, one of my favourite desserts. I had purposely had a lighter lunch so that I had room for dessert, thinking it would be okay. Well actually it wasn't okay. It spiked my blood sugar levels affecting my gestational diabetes. I had to then be monitored to see if it could be lowered, and if not, I would have to have an emergency C-section! I thought: How could I have been so stupid?! Sometimes my eyes are bigger than my belly! I should have known better. Sweet things are a big no-no for gestational diabetes. My mum and Dad happened to be visiting me and this panicked us a little bit. My mum, although concerned, was laughing a little, "You and your apple crumble." Jas on the other hand was quietly mad at me. He asked how I could be so stupid. I knew he was right, but I just hadn't been thinking straight. Another part of me was feeling that I didn't want my baby to be born on the 13th as that would mean his first birthday next year would be on Friday the 13th, and I was not having that, for sure. I think everyone knows how I feel about Friday the 13th now, considering that was the date of Luca's growth scan.

My mum told us not to focus on this and to just hope that the baby was okay. The midwife was very understanding and said she couldn't resist apple crumble either. She suggested that I have lots of water to see if that would bring my sugar levels down, and I did just that. I drank several jugs of cold water, and the nurse checked every hour to see if my levels were coming down.

When my mum and Dad left, Jas was still moaning at me for being so thoughtless. I told him that if he was just going to keep moaning, he might as well go home and that I'd be quite happy by myself drinking water and watching telly. I even said that 'The Good Wife' was going to come on soon and because it was one of my favourite programmes, I wanted to watch it in peace and quiet without Jas nagging me. As I huffed and puffed at him, my sugar levels were already starting to come down, so I told him there was nothing to worry about and that I'd see him in the morning, as planned, for the delivery of our baby.

I was relieved when Jas left because he was doing my head in. However, I know that he was concerned, and perhaps I wasn't being as patient as I should have been. Put it down to stress and overindulgence!

After 'The Good Wife' had finished at 10 o'clock, my sugar levels had come right down so everything was safe again. I decided I better get some sleep, so I put some calming music on my iPod, stuck in my earphones and hoped to drift off nicely. My head was spinning with so many thoughts though. I wondered whether everything was going to go okay; whether my baby would be well;

whether he would need to go into neonatal care and that if he did, I would feel guilty. We had pushed for this early delivery, and as much as I needed it for my own sanity, I was praying that I wasn't putting my baby in any danger. What if something happened in these last stages and he didn't make it? What if something happens to make his heart stop, just as it had with Luca? And I'm so close to having him in my arms.

I'd always been quite a positive person and looked at life with a cup half-full mentality not a cup half-empty. But after losing Luca I had become the type of person who thought the worst was always going to happen. I'd never been a paranoid person before I lost Luca, but now I couldn't ever stop focusing on the negatives. It had become a way of thinking for me, not just in relation to my baby, but with everything. Even if Jas was just a little late coming home from work, I'd wonder if he was okay or if he'd been in a car accident. I'd call him, although obviously didn't want him to answer if he was driving, which he never did since he didn't have a car phone at the time. So I would just wait and wait…and wait, and think and think – always imagining the worst case scenario.

Nothing made sense anymore, and especially statistics. For example, there's around a one percent chance that a woman will have a stillborn. However, it had happened to me! So now when anyone ever quotes this statistic, I just look at them with disgust. It happened to me and there was no cause for it! He was perfectly fine. So people can shove their statistics where the sun doesn't shine. That's how I felt when anyone threw any kind of statistic at me. This was one of the many thoughts going through my head, so consequently, I drifted in and out of sleep, and never really got a restful sleep.

The next morning, I had a shower and put on the gown that I was given, ready to be called to go down to the Delivery Theatre. Then Jas arrived with the bag of baby clothes I'd packed, and I took out what I needed. I was excited and nervous all at the same time. The anaesthetist was running late, because apparently, he'd had to attend to an emergency C-section, so understandably we had to wait a bit longer. Jas took a photo of me sitting in my chair holding my bump for the last time. We didn't talk about much; we just had the news on the TV, catching up with current affairs, although neither of us were actually listening to anything. I think we were both just alone with our thoughts about the impending arrival of our little boy.

Finally, the anaesthetist arrived, and we were ushered downstairs to the Delivery Theatre. At this point Jas and I were separated as they needed to get me ready and wired up to the machines. It was hard for them to find a vein where they could administer the canula, and then they struggled to keep me still long enough to administer the spinal injection to numb me. I don't know exactly how long this all took but once I was numb and laying on the bed, Jas came through the door in a surgical gown and took a seat next to me. He had a camera in one hand and held my hand with the other. We just looked at each other mentally saying: ‘Well, here we go. This is it now. This is the time.” We were smiling at each other because we were finally at the point that we had been waiting for all these nine months. By now, those months felt like twelve years.

At my request, the medical team didn't talk me through their procedures. I didn’t want to know all the details; I just wanted them to get on with it. It seemed to take the surgeon and his team a lot longer than I thought it would, but of course, I'd never had a C-section before, so didn't really know what to expect. I tried to remain calm. but I just couldn't help being a little anxious. Soon enough though I could feel pulling and plodding around in my stomach. It didn't hurt; I could just feel the movements. Then Jas and I finally heard a tiny cry, and we beamed from ear to ear, and shed a few tears too. It was such a joyous sound. Finally, our baby was here!

We watched as the midwife checked him over and we were full of emotion. Our baby boy cried and kicked his arms and legs as if to say: 'I'm cold!' Then the midwife placed him on my bare chest, and as soon as he heard my voice, he stopped crying. As he put his little fingers in my mouth, I said:

"Hiya, my handsome boy."

Wow, what an amazing experience that was! It was the best feeling in the world. My baby fell asleep immediately and seemed very comfortable on his mummy's chest. This just added to the amazement, joy and relief, knowing that my baby was safe and well. The midwife took a few pictures of us, which I cherish and look at quite often even now.

Then she took him from me, which I thought was much too soon. I wanted to keep him right there on my body with his heart next to mine. However, the midwife needed to do some further checks and then she'd get him dressed and bring him back to us.

In the meantime, the surgeon came to talk to us. We were in shock when he told us that the umbilical cord had been wrapped around our little baby's neck, twice, which is why it had taken them longer to get him out. The doctor continued to tell us that my placenta had also not detached very well and so they had to cut it out, which is why it took longer for them to stitch me up. This was the same thing that had happened when Luca was born, which I told the surgeon. He said it was quite normal.

We'd decided to give our baby boy the name of Ky, which we thought was a very strong sounding name. It's actually short for Kyan and means "Little King", so there's power in the name too. Whilst we waited for our baby boy to come back to us, I thought to myself: Gosh, if I hadn't insisted on Ky being born early, he may not have been here at all. Because the umbilical cord was wrapped around the baby's neck, twice, if I had gone full term, the cord would have tightened and ultimately ended his life. I closed my eyes and thanked God for the safe delivery of my child, and for answering the prayer I had written at Coventry Cathedral, almost word-for-word.

The surgeon told me that everything had been stitched up well and I hadn't lost a lot of blood, so I was okay. The midwife also assured me that all of Ky's checks had been fine. We then moved along to the recovery area where Ky was already in his little cot. I was offered a mug of tea and jam on toast, which I really needed by this time. Jas took more photos whilst I was eating, and we just couldn't stop smiling as we looked at our gorgeous little boy. He resembled Luca quite a lot, which was something else I had actually put in my prayer at the Cathedral. I didn't want him to be the spitting image of Luca but thought it would be wonderful if there was some likeness between the two brothers. God had listened to all my prayers, and I was extremely grateful and thankful.

After I had finished eating, the midwife came in and asked if I would like to feed my little baby. I was excited for this part. I had already decided that I wanted to breastfeed, so she brought Ky over to me and he latched on straight away. I couldn't help but exclaim out loud just what an incredibly awesome feeling it was. Ky was obviously very hungry, and I smiled at him as he suckled milk from my breast. The midwife smiled and told me I was doing a great job.

She came in from time to time to check the baby's temperature. It wasn't regulating quite the way it should have been, and she seemed a bit bothered by this. I asked if there was anything wrong and she said: "He should be getting warmer than he is." She decided to take him to the lamp room and put him under a warming lamp to bring his temperature up. I had never heard of a warming lamp for babies, and both Jas and I looked at one another, with some concern.

"Is he going to be okay?" I asked nervously.

She knew my history and assured us both that Ky was perfectly fine and that a drop in temperature wasn't uncommon. The midwife wheeled Ky's cot along the corridor to the lamp room, and because I was unable to walk, Jas wheeled my bed down there so we could see what the midwife was doing. She took off Ky's clothes and lay him under a large lamp. He was clearly very comfortable with this, which naturally put both Jas and I at ease. Since it was going to take fifteen minutes, the midwife suggested that Jas might want to make a few phone calls to announce the birth. The whole time I was praying quietly asking God to ensure Ky is okay!

He called my brother, Steven, first, and then our parents and his sister. Everyone was so delighted. They hadn't expected the baby to arrive so soon. We hadn't told anyone, apart from Steven, so it came as a brilliant surprise.-The family had thought that I was in hospital for a couple of days to have the steroid injections, but then would be going home.–Before Jas even got back to the room, he was receiving messages of congratulations from friends and family. News spread very quickly once it was out there.

Ky's temperature had risen very nicely, according to the midwife, so we could all go back up to my room on the Maternity Ward. I was feeling extremely exhausted. I think this was due to the sheer relief of Ky's safe arrival after being so anxious throughout the pregnancy, as well as lack of sleep the night before. In addition, the drugs that I had been given for the caesarean section were making me feel drowsy. So by this point, I wanted nothing more than to sleep. Ky was content and asleep, so it was a good time for both Jas and I to get some rest.

Jas decided to go home, and Steven was going to come and sit with me, which the midwife staff were fine with. When Steven saw Ky, he said how absolutely gorgeous he was. I knew I was biased but, of course, agreed.

You may have gathered by now that both Jas and I are major football fans. However, we support different teams – I'm an Arsenal fan and Jas supports Everton.

I'd asked Steven beforehand to bring my Arsenal scarf with him to the hospital as I wanted to take some photos of Ky with the scarf before Jas got back to the hospital, to surprise him. But he'd taken his own photos of Ky with his Everton scarf whilst I was asleep. Clearly, great minds think alike! We both wanted Ky to support our opposing teams, although we already knew which football team our son would support. In the previous March when Everton were still in the FA Cup and

Arsenal were already out of it, Jas and I made a bet. He had proposed that if Everton won the FA Cup, Ky was going to be an Everton supporter, and the backup was that whichever team finished higher up in the league that's who Ky would support. At this point Jas was convinced that Everton were going to win the FA Cup and that they would finish higher in the league than Arsenal. However, being a true 'Gooner Girl,' I knew that Arsenal would come back and I would win this bet. In true Arsenal style we did exactly that, so I had won the bet and now Ky was going to be an Arsenal supporter, well at least until he was old enough to decide for himself. Steven draped the Arsenal scarf around Ky who was fast asleep in his cot, and we took some photos. Steven then held Ky and had a few photos taken with him and the Arsenal scarf. Then it was time for me and Ky to have a nap whilst Steven went for a coffee.

I think we slept for about an hour and then the midwife came in and asked if I was ready to feed the little man again, and I replied that I was. She brought him over to me, but this time he was not latching on. She said this could happen sometimes and that maybe he just needed a little bit more skin-to-skin contact. I didn't want him to go cold again so she suggested that we just take his top layer off, and he did then latch on and took some milk.

I had missed out on lunch, so the midwife brought me a sandwich and a cup of tea. Ky seemed to have finished feeding so after I winded him, the midwife lay him down.

Then Steven and I chatted. He wanted to know all about the delivery and of course I told him that the umbilical cord had been wrapped around the baby's neck, twice, and how it could have been fatal if he'd gone full term. He was as shocked as we were, but obviously glad it all turned out well.

During this time, many midwives came in to see Ky, those from the Wellbeing Centre and also the Head Obstetrician who had given us the go-ahead to have him delivered early. I was told later that usually she doesn't make many visits, so we were very privileged. I thought it was very nice of her, and she clearly wanted to make sure we were both okay since I'd taken the risk of having Ky a little earlier than I was supposed to. They were all delighted to see that he'd arrived safe and well.

Jas had called to say he was on his way, so Steven gave me a big hug, kissed Ky on his forehead and said he'd see us the following day. I thanked my brother for coming, told him I loved him lots and thanked him for everything he'd been doing for us. He said it had been his pleasure and he loved me lots too. I feel so fortunate to have such a wonderfully supportive brother, as well as my brother, Sunny. They have both always been there for me, through thick and thin.

Soon Jas arrived and was going to be staying overnight, sleeping in the chair next to me. This had already been arranged with the Head of the Midwives, prior to the birth.

I had to drink lots of water as my sugar levels were still being monitored, and to my surprise they had already started lowering. I hadn't thought that would happen so soon after the delivery, but it was pretty much immediate. I was craving chocolate and had asked Jas to bring some, just in case I was allowed to eat it. The next time she took my blood sugars I asked the midwife if I could have a little sugar in my tea, and she said I could. So, I enquired as to whether that meant I could also have a bit of chocolate. She laughed and explained that I could, as long as it wasn't too much, and that she'd be keeping an eye on my levels. Finally, I was going to have some chocolate, and I was so happy! I'm such a chocoholic and had been the hardest thing not to eat during this pregnancy. My favourite is Cadbury's, which is what Jas had bought for me, and it was such a treat to have a couple of pieces of Dairy Milk.

Before we knew it, visiting time was close by. We had already made it clear to our parents and siblings that only they were allowed to come, no uncles, no aunties, no cousins, no-one else. We knew we were going to be there another night anyway so we said the others could come the day after. The first to arrive was Jas's mum and Dad, along with his sister. They were just beaming with pride when they saw Ky. Jas's sister said that he looked just like me. They had probably been there about ten minutes before my parents arrived. They were all in the room at the same time, which was not usually allowed, so I assumed the staff hadn't realised, or was just letting it go.

Everyone was saying how beautiful Ky was; how

blessed we were to have a baby boy and how much he resembled Luca too. It was lovely having a few family members there, all being so happy for me and Jas. Jas's sister was the first to leave and then it was just the grandparents left. They didn't want to leave too soon but they didn't want to stay too long either, because they could see that I was exhausted. My dad and Mum took quite a few photos to share with others, and I'd already sent photos to several people and had received a lot of lovely messages. Steven had asked me if I wanted him to announce the good news on Facebook. I agreed he could do this and tag me in so that all my friends could see it too. I'd had a quick look at Facebook, and we had received a huge number of congratulations.

It was just before 7:30 p.m. before our parents left and then we got settled for the evening. I had already had dinner before they had arrived and now it was time to feed Ky again before we could settle in for the night. He fed well, I burped him, and he settled back into his cot and went fast asleep. Jas made himself comfortable on the chair and I was on the bed. I was still numb from the waist down and unable to go to the bathroom, but I had a catheter which had been emptied and then reattached, so all was as well as it could be, and we could just drift off to sleep. That was easier said than done, however, as although I was exhausted, we were right next to the doors that would constantly open to take women down to the Labour Ward. I didn't want to put in my earplugs just in case I didn't hear Ky. So, it was very much a hit and miss sleep. Ky was really good in the night and slept very well. I thought this was a good start and I hoped it would continue. I had to wake him up a couple of times for feeding but he settled back down very quickly. I was getting a good couple of hours at a time. I would wake up after hearing noise, and then have to try to go back to sleep. It was like that all night long.

The next morning, I woke up feeling more refreshed than I thought I would. Ky had been great all night. Jas said that he barely heard him or the other noises on the ward. I told him I knew; I could hear him snoring through it all, and we looked at each other and laughed-

He went to get cereal and tea for us both from the breakfast trolley, and then the midwife came in to check my sugar levels, which thankfully, were now normal. She told us she'd do it once more later and then if it was still normal, then she wouldn't need to do it again.

Then it was time to feed Ky again. This time he didn't seem to be latching on properly and was fidgety, letting out a little cry as though he was still hungry. The midwife wondered if my milk flow was not coming through properly, so she did some manual checking. She was right, it wasn't coming through enough to fill him up, so we decided to manually pump some off to give to Ky with a syringe, and then we would have to top him up with formula. This seemed to work and helped him to be content, which is what we needed. She told us they'd keep a check on this whilst we were in the hospital so they could see exactly how much milk was actually coming through. She explained that sometimes it just takes a while for it to start flowing easily, but at least we had other options whilst we were the hospital. This was a relief for me knowing that Ky would be getting the good stuff from me and being topped up with formula, so I wouldn't just be giving up and going straight to formula.

I think the whole family came to see our little

man. We must have had about thirty visitors at one point. The midwife came in saying that she knew this was a very joyous time for all our family considering what we'd been through before, but there were just too many visitors, and they must leave. I asked my uncle to relay the message to everyone in the waiting area, which wasn't actually an official waiting area. That two-hour visiting time was exhausting, and Ky was a little fidgety.

Once everyone had left, I fed him and hoped he would settle, but unfortunately, he had quite an unsettled night. It was definitely not like the night before. Jas and I were up with him so much and then when he did finally sleep, so did Jas. However, I wasn't as fortunate and didn't fall asleep because Jas was snoring, and Ky was up every other hour. Consequently, I was getting an hour at a time, but the midwives on night shift were fantastic and really did help me.

The next morning, I felt as if I didn't have enough energy to even pick Ky up. I was so tired! A few checks needed to be carried out to see if there was any chance of taking Ky home. These included checking his weight, seeing if he was feeding okay, and checking on how I was doing after having a caesarean section. I was desperate to go home. I knew that if we stayed in the hospital any longer, I wouldn't sleep properly, and Ky would be more unsettled. I really wanted to get into a routine at home, in our own place, in our comfort zone.

First, Jas and I took Ky to have his weight checked. Then, as we're from an ethnic background, the midwife asked if there was any chance that anyone had been abroad who had come to visit us, as even weeks after they had returned from a foreign country they might pass on a germ or disease from that country. We didn't want Ky to pick up any bugs, so we agreed that he be given an appropriate injection to protect him, just in case.

I was still really tired and just needed to sleep for a while. Ky was settled so I lay down to sleep whilst Jas started packing the bags in the hope that we could go home. Then a midwife came by and said that we needed to take Ky back down the corridor to get his injection. I was so exhausted I literally could not lift my head off the pillow. I began to cry. Jas asked why I was crying, and I told him that I felt like a useless mother because I was too tired to take my baby for his jab. Jas hugged me and told me that I was not a useless mother, just so tired. “Don’t worry, I’ll take him for his jab. You rest. Things are going to be a lot easier once we’re home,” he assured me.

After I’d had some sleep, I told Jas that I was going to insist that I be discharged and that we all go home that day.

Jas then got the camcorder out and filmed Ky and us saying that hopefully we would be going home soon. It's so much fun to watch those films back now and hear the little cry that Ky used to make. At this point he also had a lot of phlegm in his mouth and on his chest and we put him gently on his back to get this phlegm out. It’s all on camera, but it's good stuff to show him as he's getting older. It was almost lunchtime before we got the go ahead that we could go home. We called Steven to bring the car. Jas carried Ky down the stairs, and I walked very slowly behind them.

Summary

Since I had insisted on an early delivery, I began

to worry that I might be putting my baby in danger. I was terrified that something could happen in these last stages, and he wouldn't make it. As it happened, my instincts to have Ky prematurely was the right one, because the umbilical cord had been wrapped around his neck, twice, and it could have been fatal if he'd gone full term.

Of course, it's understandable that I would be in a state of extreme anxiety before, and then after the birth, but it was exhausting dealing with the mental demons along with the physical stress. It's impossible to deny what your mind and body are experiencing during this crucial time, but I found that having Jas there with me, and being able to watch my favourite TV shows, gave me an escape from that stress. It also helped that the staff were so attentive.

It's essential that you Angel Warriors try to relax and find a way to take your minds off the negative thoughts that tend to seep into your consciousness. Easier said than done, I know, but it will help. I found that prayer was also very calming for me, and meditation can be a good way to bring your mind and body into a peaceful state.

It was obvious to us that there will be people that

are going to be sensitive, these are the ones you realise are truly there for you. And those that are just cruel, the ones you know that really couldn't care less how you are truly feeling, nor feel happy for you once you have a rainbow baby. It's a strange world we live in, people just don't know how to simply be kind!

Chapter Six

New Normal

When we arrived home, my neighbours were looking out of their windows and they waved and shouted their congratulations. We gave them a little peek of Ky in his car seat and then went inside, where we were greeted by Jas's mum and dad. They had bought some food over and just wanted to be there for when Ky arrived home. They didn't stay too long, and we really needed to catch up on our sleep and settle Ky in. I was grateful just to be back in my own home.

That night was so lovely. I felt like I was living a dream. Ky was at home with us, and we couldn't stop taking photos of him, just the three of us together. We hadn't set up our baby sensor for the cot, so all night I kept getting up to check on his every little movement and sound. It was quite painful though because of the stitches I'd had. Needless to say, the following day I got Jas to set up the baby sensor. It would put my mind at ease by monitoring Ky's heartbeat and breathing throughout the night without me having to keep jumping up to check on him. So, the baby sensor was a must in my book.

It was so lovely having Ky at home and finally having a healthy baby in my arms. I was really enjoying being a mother, bathing my baby, feeding him and doing all those things I should have been doing with Luca. The following week was the first anniversary of Luca's death and what would have been his first birthday. I always keep them separate because the 18th of June is when he died in my womb and grew his angel wings, and the 21st of June is when I gave birth to him and saw his beautiful face for the first time. So, the 21st will always remain Luca's birthday and the 18th the anniversary of his death.

A couple of people who we didn't really know that well had asked if they could come over and see Ky. The woman in the group had asked if they could come on the 21st and I'd told her that it wasn't a good day for us. I got a reply saying, "Sorry, I forgot." She went on to say, "Well at least you have another baby now, and that will help you move on." I thought no one moves on from the death of a child; another child does not replace the child you have lost. I just wanted to scream at the people who were making these comments. What were they thinking? It's one thing not being able to know what to say, but it's another to be saying stupid, insensitive and ridiculous words! I suppose in her own way she was trying to be comforting, but little did she realise just how hurtful and hollow those words were. There can be such a lack of understanding from others when a tragedy occurs, especially the loss of a child. Some people are not able to put themselves in the position of the grieving parents, because I think they're afraid to. They never want it to happen to them, so it might seem that they're in denial with their flip comments. Or maybe it's just that some people aren't born with the sympathy gene!

That particular week in June was extremely bittersweet. Only four days before Luca's anniversary, my prayers had been answered and Ky, my beautiful healthy baby boy, was in my arms. It was such a blessing that he was home with us at such a difficult time – it would have been so much harder without him.

Luca's first birthday was extremely emotional. My son was having his first birthday in heaven, and not with us, where we would have been throwing a big party for him. I could not hug him, kiss him, hold him, shower him with my love and gifts. Instead, I bought a small cake, put a number one candle on it and his photo next to it and Jas and I blew out the candle together. Afterwards we both held Ky and cried tears of sorrow and joy.

Jas was off work on paternity leave for a total of three weeks, and during that time we had built a routine that we could continue when Jas went back to work. It was lovely having that time together, something we had waited to have for so long. We were sharing duties, which made me a little worried about how I would cope once he was back at work. Back then we didn't have a dishwasher because it seemed like a luxury we didn't need. However, when Ky was six months old, and after I won the poker match at our family Christmas games, we decided to buy a dishwasher. Washing all the baby bottles was so much easier after that, and I kicked myself for not getting a dishwasher sooner.

The midwife visited to check on Ky and thankfully he was putting on the weight he'd lost and was thriving. This was extremely reassuring, as it would be for any parent.

We didn't allow lots of people to come and see Ky and made a decision that those who would be able to meet him were those who had supported us when Luca had died. Then we realised that as there were so many people asking to see Ky, that we would have, what East Indians call, a Kheer party. This is a party to celebrate the birth of a child, and is similar to a christening, but without the blessing. We decided it would take place just after Ky was eight weeks old, and after he'd had all of his jabs. We hired the Community Hall in our village and booked caterers for 120 people. Jas's parents had paid for the food, and we paid for everything else, including alcohol. So, the drinks were flowing and everyone was in a mighty good mood celebrating the birth of Ky. Music was played from my iPod through a loud-speaker, and there was plenty of dancing.

A week before the party we had beautiful photos of the three of us taken by a professional photographer. He took some lovely ones of Ky in very cute poses - such as in a basket with blankets and wearing little hats. Some of these were taken whilst he was awake but a lot when he was asleep. I cherish those photos, which are proudly displayed in our home. They're my absolute favourite photos of Ky when he was a baby.

He was wonderful throughout the party. He stayed asleep in his pushchair for most of it and only woke up for a feed and a nappy change. I was pleased that he slept, as I didn't want everyone holding him and possibly spreading germs. As you can tell, I was very protective of my little boy, and quite the "Tiger Mum!"

Jas was so out of it, having had his fair share of alcohol with so many celebratory cheers on the birth of his son, that he didn't notice any of this happening.

When we got home, I had to get Jas to bed, which was quite funny, whilst Ky was lying in his cot awake and kicking, making up for all the sleep he'd had during the day.

The next day, Jas was hungover and not feeling great, understandably. I filled him in with the things he could remember haha. A few weeks later my cousin Karen had a baby girl, so beautiful.

We were enjoying being a little family and soon

we were looking forward to Ky's first Christmas, which was amazing. He was dressed as a little Santa and was spoilt with love and gifts by the whole family. We were all together at my parents' home where we all grew up. Time was flying by now that we had our handsome little Ky in our lives.

As I had been made redundant from my job in project management just before Ky was due to be born, I was able to have eighteen months off with him, which was fantastic and a proper start to motherhood with my little baby. I loved seeing all the changes, and there were lots of mile-stones that I was there for, such as his first words. It was a very exciting period.

During this time, the legal case we had started regarding Luca's medical negligence, continued. One independent midwife had stated she believed there was negligence involved, but the independent obstetrician thought that there hadn't been and said there was no guarantee that Luca would have survived. As he had the final say, the case came to a close with no justice for Luca. I was fuming, I wanted a third person to make a decision. This was completely unfair and unfounded in our eyes. The solicitor said we could carry on with the case but would need to pay. Sadly, we didn't have the money to carry on with it. Surely it made sense to get another verdict if one witness says 'yes' and the other says 'no', but apparently that's not how it works. Even with the facts they had about Ky's growth scan, which was almost identical to Luca's, and the fact that I was put on weekly and eventually daily scanning with Ky, didn't matter. Surely if they had done that with Luca, they would have noticed he had stopped growing at some point and that they needed to get him out, after which I believe he would have survived.

To us, it was complete and utter negligence that had caused the loss of our son, and there was now nothing we could do about it. We were heartbroken that there was no justice for Luca, and even more so that the midwife who had missed the warning signs on his growth scan could be doing this to more families. I wanted to stop her, but now I was helpless to do so.

Eventually as my statutory maternity pay stopped, we were struggling financially. I knew I wanted to go back to work, and that nursery would be good for Ky. He was so clingy with me and it would be a great way for him to start socialising with others. I started looking for work after his first birthday, which had been lovely. We had a little party for him in the Community Hall in our village again, with just children from our closest family and our friends' children. We kept it to young children under seven. It didn't cost very much and was simply a children's party with nothing much for the adults, in contrast to the party we'd had when Ky was born. It turned out very well.

Some months before someone, had told me some insensitive things that had been said by yet another person about Luca and moving on. This caused an argument between Jas and I, he couldn't understand why I would take comments to heart so much. During which, I finally, I spat out the words I had been holding onto for so long, "How would you feel if Luca had died in your arms? Well, he died inside my body, and that will stay with me forever!!" In that moment Jas finally got it, and we both held each other and cried. Ky was in his cot awake but, luckily, kicking away oblivious to what was happening between his parents,

All of this had put me into a depression, so in February of 2014, I sought help from my GP who prescribed antidepressants. I was still grieving for Luca and wanted to be the best mum I could be for Ky, but it was all very overwhelming, and had started to affect my marriage.

A few weeks after taking the antidepressants I started to feel better. When my GP asked how things were going, I told him that I knew it might sound strange, but I was starting to love my husband again. We both laughed, and he told me that was an excellent sign. Then I knew I was on the right track by taking the pills. Also, since we were no longer seeing the insensitive people, we were now in a much better place in our marriage.

My mom knew that we were struggling financially and that I was looking for a job, but she desperately wanted me to stay at home as long as I could with Ky. So, my parents gave us some money so that I could be off a little longer, and not have to stress about finances. By this time, I had enrolled Ky into our local nursery and went with him at first to get him settled into the new environment. I was applying for jobs but obviously didn't know when one would come up, so it was the sensible thing to get Ky settled at the nursery where he would be full time once I took up a new role.

In November 2014, I was due to be at an interview for a large corporate company. A few days before the interview I came down with laryngitis and had to email the agency to let them know I could not attend. They questioned whether I was serious about attending the interview and I told them I absolutely was but couldn't be at an interview if I couldn't talk. Luckily, it was rearranged for about ten days later. I had two interviews all on the same day, one with the person who would be my line manager, and the other with the person who would be my department manager. The interviews went very well and the following afternoon I found out that I had got the job. They wanted me to start a week before Christmas just to get the nitty gritty out of the way, so that I could start my full role in the New Year. I said I would have to check when the nursery could take Ky full time, as that was the biggest part of the equation. In addition, because the nursery closed over Christmas, I would not be able to work all days over the Christmas period, as Jas was also working some of the days too. We came to some compromises and the nursery luckily said that they could take Ky the week before Christmas as many children would already be going home and starting their Christmas holidays with their parents. That was extremely fortunate timing for us.

In the couple of weeks leading up to starting my full-time job, I was taking Ky into nursery for full days twice a week so he would get used to it. When I started my job, it felt quite daunting as I hadn't worked since Luca had died. But I soon got my feet under the table and settled into the job pretty quickly. Everyone was so nice, which made it even better.

Now that we were going to have two incomes, we splashed out a little bit over Christmas and bought more presents than we would normally. Jas had been wanting a Samsung tablet for quite a while so that is what I got from his boys for Christmas. We have always made a point of making sure Luca is part of our Christmases and any occasions in-between, such as birthdays, Mother's Day, and Father's Day. Sometimes we'd receive a present from each of our boys, but sometimes it's been something big from both of them. No matter what, we have always made sure Luca's included, which we'll continue to do for the rest of our lives.

This was now Ky's second Christmas, and he was obviously more interested in tearing the paper off the presents than the presents themselves. He got lots of toys and some clothes, which he just threw across the room as any eighteen-month-old child would do. We had bought him a little battery-operated toy dog that barked and walked. I thought he would love it because he liked dogs, but he hated it and was actually quite scared of it. Eventually he warmed towards the toy dog, and still loves it to this day.

It was a quiet, cosy Christmas at home, which was just what we needed. Normally we would all get together at my mum and Dad's house in Leicestershire, but this time they came to us with my brother, Steven.

Naturally, all the focus was on Ky because he was a funny little character. He loved laughing at silly things and noises, and everyone just wanted to be holding and cuddling this chubby, cute little fella. This year he was dressed as an elf for Christmas and looked just as cute as he did the previous year, when he was Santa.

He got quite a kick out of taking selfies of himself in his elf outfit, while I held the phone, of course.

The next day was a nice lazy Boxing Day at home, just Jas, Ky and me. Jas and I did this every year, but this one I've never forgotten as it was when Ky started walking by himself. I was giddy with excitement seeing him walk from room to room on his own. It was a lovely sight.

Slowly but surely we had now reached a point where we were beginning to live again. It was not that we had got over the loss of Luca - as I've said, no parent ever gets over the loss of their child, but we had started to enjoy life again since Ky had been born. The antidepressants had played a part in this as well, and I was now getting my focus back.

Also, once I had started work, I began to feel a bit like the old me again. I knew I would never fully be that person again because a big part of me died when I lost Luca, but I was in a good place and that was a great feeling. I knew now that I didn't need the antidepressants, so I saw my GP and told him that I wanted to come off them, which I realised would be a slow, gradual process.

Jas and I also decided we wanted to take a holiday. This would be our first holiday since going to Rome after Luca died. Now it was going to be just the three of us. So, it had to be a child and family friendly place with a beach. We found the perfect spot - Puerto Rico in Gran Canaria – and after I got my first pay cheque in January, we booked our holiday.

We stayed in an apartment suite holiday complex near the marina and just a couple of minutes' walk to the beach and restaurants. It was wonderful. Ky was great on the flight and slept most of the way there, and on the way back. We thoroughly enjoyed our holiday, and in fact, we've been back there every year since. We always go for two weeks in June, for Ky's birthday. The locals know us by now, and they've seen Ky grow up.

On Luca's birthday we always go to the place where we scattered his ashes, as a way of visiting him. We have a cake for him, and I kiss a balloon and send it off into the sky for him to catch. Also, every year on Mother's Day, I post something on Facebook, referring to my two gorgeous boys.

In the first few months after Ky started nursery, he was constantly catching bugs and getting colds, tonsillitis etc. We'd been warned that this was common, so Jas and I often had to take it in turns looking after our sick child since we were both full-time working parents. By the end of March 2015, going into early April, thankfully all this began to stop, and it was great to have that respite.

We had booked another holiday for Ky's second birthday, but this time we went to Portugal. It was beautiful, and we had a great holiday, but it wasn't as nice as Gran Canaria. I think when you find somewhere that you love so much, it's hard to beat it and when you have set the bar high, you now compare everything to that one place that was just magical. That's why we decided to go back to Gran Canaria after that.

As we were still off for another week, we took a few day trips with Ky and obviously went to Luca's resting place. It is so peaceful and beautiful along the river, in a very quiet village of Leicestershire. Then we came home, cut a cake for Luca and kissed a bio-balloon to send to the sky.

That year we also had my brother Steven's wedding. He was marrying his girlfriend, Grace, and I was so looking forward to their wedding. The wedding was set for August. Jas and I had decided we were going to try for another baby, but I said let's put off trying until after Steven's wedding as I wanted to be able to enjoy it without being in the early stages of pregnancy. So, we agreed that I would come off the contraceptive pill in preparation, which is what I did.

Work was great and I was fully settled into the tech company. There were so many projects, but it was very enjoyable as well as being nice and flexible. I worked for one day at home and four days in the office. Jas also did this, and on the days we worked from home, we were able to collect Ky earlier from nursery, which was really nice.

Suddenly Steven's wedding was upon us and we were all very excited. Ky looked so cute in his waistcoat and cravat. Grace looked stunning and Steven was so handsome in his tuxedo; my little brother, the baby of the family was getting married! At other weddings, and parties, before Luca died, I'd be on the dance floor non-stop, but some part of that had died in me. Although I thoroughly enjoyed the wedding, I wasn't constantly on the dance floor, so this was different for me. There were times when I'd just go off and look after the children who were all playing together; then I'd go back when some of my favourite songs were playing. The D.J. was great! He was mixing in R&B, hip hop beats as well as bhangra tunes, and the atmosphere on the dance floor was electric. it was the best wedding ever!

I had a couple of days off work after the wedding as I knew I needed time to recuperate for all the partying. I still sent Ky to nursery and it was lovely having a bit of time to myself.

Work was fantastic, getting better and better all the time. I was now working a lot for the directors of the IT Department, reporting directly to one director in particular and involved with other departments on lots of projects. This was a great position to be in, but It didn't stop my wants and desires for another child, so Jas and I started trying for a baby.

I always see work as a way to live, I don't live to work. Ever since I started working as a trainee cashier for a bank when I was sixteen, I've thought of myself as a career minded person. So much so that I've built my way up to being a project manager, constantly aiming high and studying along the way. I'd managed to get where I wanted to be. I was happy and content with my career path, my only next step from here would have been senior project manager. However, the job I really wanted was to be the mother of another baby.

Summary

No matter what other people say, having another child does not and never will take the pain away of the loss of your child. A new child definitely does not replace your other child either. What it does do, is give you someone else to love and to focus your attention on. This helps towards building your life again, whilst you still carry the grief within you.

Being a good Christian, I believe in giving people more chances than they deserve in order to right themselves. However, as some ministry programmes teach, sometimes you also need to know when to walk away. I did that with certain people in my life, but Jas also decided to do the same.

I have found over the years that grief is like an inflatable backpack. Sometimes, it is full and heavy with grief, other times less so, but it is always there. You grieve for your own flesh and blood, the baby you loved from the very beginning of inception, and all the plans and life you were meant to have together. It seems as if Mother Nature has played a cruel trick...and so, you grieve.

I feel for children who have lost a parent at a young age too. Parents are meant to be around to help nurture their child well into full adulthood, and then to see the birth of their grandchildren. I'd always felt like that from when Princess Diana had died and seeing Prince William and Harry at her funeral was deeply upsetting and still is if I ever see those images now.

Now when I hear of someone passing at the age of eighty or above, I think: I'm glad they lived a full life. As sad as it is that they have gone and will be dearly missed, I think of the lives they must have had, the stories they could tell, and the legacy they've left behind.

Chapter Seven

Best Laid Plans

Being a full-time working mum and a project manager in a role which was extremely taxing at times, I was starting to feel very tired. I'd always loved my sleep, so I thought maybe it was just that my body wasn't getting as much rest as it needed. Just to be on the safe side though, since we have cases of anaemia in my family, I decided to go to the doctor to get checked out. Everything was fine, which I was glad to hear, and he suggested it was probably due to the hustle and bustle of life that comes with being a full-time working mum.

I was being pulled into more and more projects while Jas and I were still trying for a baby. It wasn't happening as quickly as it had previously with Luca and Ky, when it had been immediate. This was starting to play on my mind a little bit. I was wondering if maybe now that I was almost forty, I was getting to the age when it was not going to be as easy to get pregnant as it had been.

We had great news though that Steven and Grace were expecting their first child. Steven told us the news in November 2015, a honeymoon baby for sure. I thought: 'well, I'll get pregnant soon and the babies will grow up together.' I was over the moon for them.

As we came to 2016, after a lovely Christmas at my mum and Dad's with my brothers and their wives, we had a quiet New Year at home, which we have done every year now since Luca passed away.

In March 2016 I turned forty, and we went back to Gran Canaria for my birthday and thoroughly enjoyed it, as we always did. I was spoilt by everybody at work and at home and by friends. It was a beautiful milestone birthday. Jas and I have the same birthday, but this birthday was all about me because it was my fortieth. He is two years younger than me.

Although work was busy and I was in a good place working with the directors on important projects, that March I had been expecting a big bonus and a pay rise; however, that did not happen. Not only was I disappointed, but many of my colleagues who had been expecting the same rewards for their hard work, were as well. It was disheartening to think that I'd got so far in my career and wasn't getting a pay rise or a bonus. It turned out that the company wasn't doing as well as they should have been. Then I was surprised when my line manager told me that I would still get a pay rise to recognise my hard work; so that made me happy. This was done via a kind of nomination scheme of certain colleagues whose names were pinned onto a board – the equivalent of names in a hat, I suppose. I knew my name was floating about, and all the directors knew me, so surely after pulling off some very hard projects that others were not able to manage, then I was definitely a person they surely would reward. Sadly, this again did not happen, and because I certainly wasn't being valued, around June 2016, I started looking for another job

I came across a job in the finance sector – at a Building Society - which was an area I had wanted to get into. I also thought it would be good just to get some interview practice. There was a building society headquarters near where I lived and this is where I ultimately wanted to be working, but they didn't have any positions available at the time. However, I thought if I could get a job at another building society, at least I'd get my foot in the door. The job was located straight down an 'A' road about thirty-five minutes from where we lived; consequently, the journey time would be a little bit shorter than where I was currently. The interview went well, and I was offered the position. It was twenty percent more money than I was earning currently, and I was offered a car allowance too. Although it ticked many of the boxes that I was looking for, there was still some travel time, but it wasn't that bad. Since I thought it could be a very good fit for me, I decided to take it after discussing it with Jas. Also, as there was only a three-month probation period, even if I did get pregnant within that time, it would be fine. Or we could even just wait until the New Year before we tried for a baby again.

During this period, I'd also had checks carried out to make sure that I was still able to get pregnant. Everything had come back fine, although my thyroid level was slightly high. Even though I was still within the normal range, being on the higher side can sometimes stop a woman from conceiving.

So, the specialist prescribed Levothyroxine to treat my elevated thyroid.

I handed in my notice at the IT company at the end of August 2016, but because I was still owed annual leave, this shortened the amount of my notice. They were sad to see me go, but since they couldn't match the salary that I was being offered at the building society, I ultimately had to leave. I was given a very nice send off and initially kept in touch with some of the people I was working with, but as often happens, eventually we ended up losing touch.

Before starting the new job, I had a particularly good detox with Forever Living C9. It was brilliant. I lost seven pounds within nine days, which was a very good start, and I was feeling in a good place to continue trying for a baby. That September I also added Luca to our surname so that his name would live on forever, through us. We now have a double- barrel name, although I am more commonly known as Sharon Luca. At first it was just me and Ky because Jas wasn't sure, but he did eventually do it too. I started the new job with Luca in my surname which was a lovely feeling. However, when starting a new job, people want to get to know you and some asked if I was Italian. I explained that Luca was actually my first son who was stillborn, and we've added his name to our surname so that he lives on with us. They found that to be so lovely and touching and a really nice way to remember Luca. It was hard to keep having to tell the same story and eventually I started feeling anxious every time I was asked. To help me with this, the doctor gave me a very low dosage of antidepressants Starting any new job can be daunting, so there was a little bit of pressure there too.

I was thrilled when a couple of weeks later I was given a glowing review for my first month in the job. I also realised that I didn't really need the antidepressants; everything was fine, and things had settled down.

I was enjoying the new job and the project I'd been assigned. it had given me a different set of challenges which I was up for. I've always been career motivated and liked a challenge. Also, the people I was working with within this group were fantastic; we had a great rapport.

At the end of November on my way to work in my Volkswagen Tiguan SUV, whilst stationary at a roundabout, I was hit by a small Corsa from behind. The driver was a young woman who'd been on her mobile phone. I'd been jolted forward in the car, which had caused damage to the bumper underneath the plastic cover, although at the time I couldn't see any damage. When I got out of the car, the woman was quite abrupt and shouting that there was no damage to my car and that everything was fine. I said that I needed to take her details, nonetheless. I also took a photo of her number plate, just in case she'd given me false details. She didn't like this at all. Arriving late at work, I apologised to my manager and explained what had happened. One of my colleagues could see that I was a bit shaken and took me to the canteen and made me a mug of sweet tea.

Later that afternoon, I started to get pain in my neck, and my manager said I should go home since I might have whiplash. He also advised me to make an appointment to see my doctor if it got any worse. I phoned my insurance company to let them know that I had been involved in an accident that morning, and I gave the details of the woman who had crashed into the back of my car. They arranged for my car to be seen at a Volkswagen registered body shop. It was then that we found out that the bumper was damaged underneath and needed to be repaired. The following day I was in a lot of pain, so I went to the doctor who confirmed I had whiplash and he gave me pain medication. I was unable to go into work, and since I was still within my three-month probation period, wouldn't have got paid if I had gone off sick. Fortunately, because the project hadn't fully taken off yet, it was easy for me to do light work at home. I attended to my emails, but nothing much beyond that. Consequently, I was able to rest and still send Ky to nursery. This went on until the New Year.

That Christmas I was in a lot of pain and could hardly move. I'd thought the whiplash would be gone or at least have eased up by the time Christmas came, but it didn't seem to be going anywhere. I did struggle not being able to do as much for Ky as I would normally have. The week in between Christmas and New Year I became very poorly with a full on cold and fever. I felt awful. We had arranged to meet up with friends, Rosie and Jessa, and their husbands and children at Rosie's house. I'd met these lovely ladies through our husbands who had been friends since school and college days, and we'd become extremely good friends, best friends, like sisters really. Our children were all similar ages, and they had also become friends growing up together. As I was unwell, Jas went with Ky and they had a great time. I lay on the sofa, binge-watched Suits on Netflix, drank lots of fluids and slept.

After the New Year, I went to work for the first time since the accident and was in horrific pain driving there. The company had moved offices and were now in Banbury, which was over an hour away, each way. I soon realised that I couldn't carry on living with the pain, and I needed to seek extra help. My manager could see how I was struggling and advised me to make an appointment with a physiotherapist as soon as possible. She also told me that I could work from home for a couple of days a week since the project still wasn't at full throttle. I would need to be in the office at least twice a week, and even though it was extremely painful for me to drive, it was something I had to do for my job. I started seeing a physiotherapist, but the pain was now becoming more widespread. It wasn't just in my neck and shoulders, it was also in my back, my hips and at the top of my legs; sometimes it would also radiate down my arms. In addition, I was getting horrific headaches at times, and all I wanted to do was lie down. I couldn't believe a small accident had caused so much pain.

Jas thought it would do me good to get away into some heat rather than the cold we were experiencing at home. So, he booked a holiday to our favourite place, Gran Canaria, and was right - the heat did me good. Unfortunately, when I returned to the cold, I was back at square one again.

The work project was now ramping up, and my manager needed me in the office a lot more. This meant that decisions had to be made, especially since I was in so much pain. I was in tears after my meeting with the manager, which led to a mini breakdown. Not great for this to take place at the office, but I was in a side office by myself and no-one saw me. I had to message one of my friends in the office to bring me some tissues. When she saw how upset I was, she told me that I couldn't carry on the way I was and needed help. I'd previously told my manager that I had depression and she said that I didn't look depressed. I thought that was such a ridiculous thing to say.

How can you tell if someone's depressed? It was certainly not what I needed to hear then especially when my whole body was in so much pain. Saying what she did definitely tipped me over and made me start crying, but mainly I was crying because of all the pain I was feeling. I was aware that I needed to do more at work, but I didn't know how I was going to do that when driving into the office was causing me more and more pain every time I travelled.

My friend suggested I talk to the Head of the Department who was my manager's manager and see what she thought. It took me several attempts to get myself back together, whilst my friend called the Department Head. When she eventually arrived, she could see how upset I was, and said that obviously my depression had got worse with all the pain. She suggested that I take sick leave and get myself checked out properly, without having to worry about travelling, the project or anything else. She said the company would support me for as long as it took and told me to take it month by month and do whatever I needed to get better.

I already had an appointment with my GP the following day because I needed to get some more painkillers, and he signed me off sick. He didn't increase my antidepressant medicine because he wanted to see how I got on that first month - see if anything improved.

I had a month off work, and whilst it slowly started to get warmer here in Warwickshire, I wasn't getting any better in terms of pain, and I was still depressed. I was starting to see different doctors recommended by the solicitors my insurance company had appointed after the car accident. However, it soon became clear that the body pain I was experiencing, although still related to the accident, was no longer whiplash, but something else. One of the doctors suggested I see a chiropractor, and after a few sessions she could tell that there was something wrong with my neck. She thought it might be a bulging disc, and the only way to find this out would be by having a scan. She then contacted my G.P. and suggested he refer me for an MRI.

Thankfully, my employers were still paying me; also, a woman in Human Resources told me that I had Bupa private insurance coverage, and she gave me a number to contact to arrange an appointment at a private hospital. It was now August and I'd been off work for five months.

Within a space of three weeks, I saw a rheumatologist, had an MRI and was diagnosed with arthritis in my neck, a bulging disc and fibromyalgia, a chronic pain disease which can be triggered by a trauma such as a car accident. Fibro, as it is known for short, affects the whole body, as well as bringing on fatigue. It now made sense why my body was always in pain and why I was so tired. Once I had this diagnosis, Jas felt quite guilty for having called me lazy a few months earlier as all I ever wanted to do was sleep. Unfortunately, as there is no cure for fibromyalgia, I was told the only thing that I could do was to learn to manage it. I was referred to a pain management clinic as well as for CBT - cognitive behavioural therapy - to help me come to terms with my diagnosis and understand how to live within my limitations, which would eventually become more and more evident. I was also given more medication to help me manage the pain, but as the cold months set in, the pain increased.

By Christmas I was full of pain but was still learning how to manage my new way of life. How strange it was that I had to learn a new way of life, yet again - first when Luca had died, and now with this chronic illness. I felt defeated and couldn't understand what was going to become of my life. Ky had started school in the previous September and was in the Reception Class, so my days were spent resting. Sometimes, because I was on so many medications, I'd be out of it and asleep most of the time. I had to set my alarm to go and pick up Ky from school. I couldn't quite understand how my life had changed so radically since the accident; from being someone who was physically active: doing yoga, boxercise and spinning classes, to not being able to do anything at all.

Christmas and New Year came and went. Then in January when Ky was five and a half, he asked me how Luca had died. Even though I knew one day this question would come, it nonetheless took me by surprise. It came out of the blue; we hadn't even been talking about Luca. We were just watching television and suddenly Ky asked me about his brother.

I'd remembered what my mum had said to me when I was a child after my great grandfather had died, and I said,

"His heart stopped working, Ky, and now he's in a happy place in the sky."

He thought about it for a while, then said, "In the sky?"

I told Ky that I believed that when we die, we go to a beautiful place in the sky where it's sunny, warm and happy all day long.

"What about at night?"

"That's when the stars come out to play," I told him. "Next time you see a star, you can say 'hello Luca' and his star will shine like the brightest diamond in the sky."

It's very difficult to explain death to a child, and based on Ky's question about his brother, I was inspired to write an illustrated children's book entitled: 'Why Did Grandad Die?' It expands on the conversation I had with Ky, and I hope will give parents and teachers another way of explaining the loss of a loved one to a child.

I was still employed, although no longer being paid, and was determined to find a way to get back to work in this New Year. My employer and I looked at different ways I could work from home. However, being a full-time project manager was not ideal. Plus, with the brain fog I experienced with fibromyalgia, I wasn't sure I wanted to go straight back into a full-time project management role. I needed something else to ease me in. There was an office in Leicester which would be nearer for me to get to and not be such a long drive, but unfortunately there were no jobs there, not even part-time. After a few meetings with my employers, it became clear that I would not be able to return to work, and I was let go on the basis of poor health.

This was four days before my birthday and Jas's fortieth, so not a fantastic start to that week. Fortunately, I had saved up a bit of money from when I was being paid during the first six months I was off work, so Jas and I decided we'd go to Dubai for five nights. My parents had gone on a tour of India and Kerela, and on their way back they stopped off in Dubai, so they were there for a couple of nights with us. They enjoyed being able to have a day out with Ky, which is something they'd never really done before. We all went to the Underwater Zoo at the Dubai Mall on the day of our birthdays and had a lovely time together. It was a fantastic holiday and it really perked me up.

Summary

It's interesting how just when you think you've got it all figured out, something can come along and literally knock the wind out of you. Jas and I were beginning to enjoy life with Ky, I was working in a job I loved, and we were planning for another baby. Life was beginning to look good. Then the car accident changed all that. It didn't seem fair, that I'd suffered so much emotional pain when I lost Luca, and now I was experiencing great physical pain. At times it was difficult for me to figure it all out, and I still haven't, not completely anyway. I do take strength from Ky. He literally motivates me to get out of bed in the morning when my body is screaming: "No!" And, of course, Jas is my rock.

No matter what life throws at us, it is up to us to face the challenges head on and somehow know that we will overcome…we will survive because we are Angel Warriors!

Inspiration can come from the most unusual

places, so we need to always be open and be prepared when it arrives. Out of the blue one day, my son, Ky, suddenly wanted to know how Luca had died. I had to take a deep breath, because it was a very important question and I didn't want to make a mistake. I thought about what my mother had told me when my granddad had died, and then I searched for the right words to explain death to my five-year old son. Based on this somewhat difficult conversation with Ky, it occurred to me that there didn't seem to be much literature out there to explain death to a child. This was when the idea of an illustrated children's book came into my mind. I decided to call it "Why Did Granddad Die?" and based it on my conversation with Ky.

I believe that we can be presented with opportunities to turn a negative into a positive. We just have to be willing to accept even the glimmer of an idea that may be a way of honoring the memory of the child we have lost, and may also make a difference in the lives of others.

Chapter Eight

Growing Pains

After Easter I developed sciatica. This is a symptom of fibromyalgia and something I'd never had before. The pain was really awful and made me cry. I couldn't walk properly and needed a walking stick. This continued for many weeks into June and over Ky's birthday. It was also the 6th anniversary of Luca's death, and for the first time on this occasion I was alone. Ky was at school and Jas was at work. Luca's birthday hit me like a tsunami and came out of nowhere. I think there were many reasons for this though - not just that it was the anniversary of Luca's death, but also that I was crippled with pain, was still getting used to managing my illness, had lost my career and didn't know what my future held.

It was just too much and caused a complete and utter breakdown. I sobbed uncontrollably and screamed into pillows. It was as if Luca had just died again, and the pain was so fresh. All the tears, sadness and heartbreak put me into what is called 'fibro flare'. This is when your body becomes so exhausted that you have no alternative but to take to your bed, which was what I did... for almost a full week.

On the day of my breakdown, I was in no state to be able to pick Ky up from school, so I asked my friend, whose daughter was in the same class as Ky, if she could drop Ky off at home. She knew exactly why, and when she arrived at the front door, I dropped to my knees and flung my arms around Ky. My friend said that he was exactly what I'd been waiting for all day, and I agreed. She could read me like a book, but I suppose any mother would be able to understand that moment whilst you're grieving for one child and all you really want is to wrap your arms around your other child too, or several children as the case may be. I knew there would be no other children for us though. Since the car accident, which had resulted in my excruciating pain, Jas and I had stopped trying for another baby.

After the week of Ky's birthday and Luca's anniversary and birthday, as if I didn't have enough to deal with, I twisted the knee of my right leg. I didn't feel it immediately as I was already in so much pain from the sciatica, which radiated down my leg. I now always needed a walking stick. It wasn't until my knee swelled up like a balloon that I knew something was wrong. In the last week of June/early July I made an appointment with the pain management clinic who said it could be due to fibromyalgia but advised that if it didn't calm down in a couple of weeks, that I should go and see my GP. By the end of July, the sciatica had subsided, but my knee was still extremely painful and swollen so off I went to my GP who referred me for an MRI scan.

Before I had twisted my knee, we had booked to go back to Gran Canaria for the last week of August, before school started again. I wasn't quite sure how I was going to manage with my knee being so bad but there's no way we could cancel, and the MRI wasn't actually going to happen until early September, after the holiday. At the airport, as I was classified as 'disabled' due to the fact that I had a walking stick, they helped me jump the queues so that I could then sit down as soon as possible.

In Gran Canaria it felt as if we were having two separate holidays; Jas and Ky would go off during the day to the beach, into town or to the parks etc., whilst I lay on a sunbed near the pool of the apartment suites. I was hoping if I went in the pool, it would help my knee, but it didn't. Jas and Ky always joined me at the poolside after they'd had their day out and they enjoyed splashing around in the pool while I watched. I felt like I was missing out on having a good holiday with Ky, but he was having a lot of fun with his dad. I thought: 'It is what it is, and I'll just make the most of what I can do,' even though it wasn't much.

Fortunately, because of the warm weather in Gran Canaria and previously in England, all my other aches and pains had become a lot easier to deal with. Also, as the streets were mostly level, it wasn't hard for me to walk to a restaurant in the evening with Jas and Ky.

So all in all, I managed okay and did feel rested.

When we got home, I had the MRI on my knee. I was still in agonising pain whilst I waited the three to four weeks to get my results, but I instinctively knew it wasn't due to fibromyalgia. The pain with fibro is quite different to what I was experiencing with my knee – it's a dull nagging pain all over the body and is constant. Some days it's easier than others, but nonetheless, it's always there. Anyone who's ever had a twisted knee which turned out to be a grade two sprain, will know how painful it is. After finally getting my results, the doctor said it would probably be best if I had a cortisone injection. However, this was going to be administered at the doctor's surgery by a GP, trained to do it, and would take place at the end of October during half term week. Jas had taken part of that week off, so the timing was good. He drove me to the appointment and because there was no one for us to leave Ky with, he came too. What a mistake that was! Lots of people who'd previously had cortisone shots told me it would be fine, and I wouldn't really feel it. They were lying! The injection was extremely painful; it was like having an epidural during childbirth. It hurt <u>so</u> much, and I let out an almighty scream! The doctor said she'd never had anyone react quite like that when having a steroid injection, and realised it was the fibromyalgia that was making me hypersensitive to it. In the past, needles never bothered me, but I'd become hypersensitive to needles since I'd developed fibro. Ky got scared because I was screaming, and I felt extremely guilty that he was there. I reassured him that I was okay even though I had tears in my eyes. Needless to say, when we were back home, he was constantly asking me if I was okay. I was devastated that my poor baby had to see his mummy experiencing such torture. I silently cursed those people who had told me that I wouldn't feel anything, when it had been completely the opposite.

The pain actually got worse after the steroid injection. I ended up in bed for quite a number of days, so I missed out on half term with Ky. Luckily, Jas was off work, so they were able to do things together. Yet again another holiday with Ky off school where I was missing out on having fun with him.

I was trying to walk without my walking stick, and even though I was okay to do short distances, I just wasn't able to go very far at all. As much as I wanted to look around the shops, this was absolutely out of the question. So I was given a 'disabled' blue badge.

At this time, I was also having physio to get my anterior cruciate ligament (ACL) strong again and make the knee stronger overall. For some reason the physio aggravated the knee. We didn't really know why.

Winter was now upon us, and every single part of my body was in so much pain, not only with my knee, but with the fibromyalgia. It was excruciating! I cried on Jas's shoulder, "I can't go on like this." We decided that it was time to see a private chiropractor and I made an appointment as soon as I could with someone who had been recommended. It turned out that the kneecap had somehow moved out of place, and the chiropractor was going to have to slowly move it back. Because of the fibro, it couldn't be done all in one go, so she could only do a fifth of the amount of work on me than she would do on a normal healthy person. There had to be quite a number of sessions. It turns out that my hip was not aligned, which was also causing a problem down my leg and I was putting more pressure on my knee. She explained that if my foot was on the brake at the time of the accident, this would have caused my hip alignment to be moved, which then had a knock-on effect on that side. It's always my right side. The sciatica was on my right side, my twisted knee was the right leg, not to mention all the back pain, neck pain and shoulder pain. I was a walking bag of pain.

We were nearly a year on now, since the knee

problem and my chiropractor suggested that there was probably something more going on. She said I needed to have another MRI scan, which I had at a private hospital. It showed that I had cartilage damage, but the knee structure itself was fine. It was the fibro that was causing so much pain there. I recently found out that as fibromyalgia is such a complex illness, if you are severely injured like I was with my knee, the brain signals to that area and will keep it in constant pain.

There is no cure or operation that can stop this. After seeing three consultants, the diagnosis was not very satisfactory. I was told that there was never going to be a cure for my knee and that I would probably never be able to walk properly again. The only thing they could try, which I'm still waiting for to this day, is to have three of the six nerves in my knee blocked with nerve blocker. This will send signals to my brain to lessen the pain. Hopefully, I will then be able to exercise my knee and strengthen it to the point where I can start walking unaided again. This is an extremely long process and there's no guarantee that it will even work. Consequently, I now have to accept that I am a person with limitations. I have to focus on what I can do with the strength that I do have, which is not very much, unfortunately. Having a 'normal' life and being able to kick around a football with my son as I did before all this happened, is looking extremely unlikely, but I never lose hope. I've always been an optimistic person and try to look for the silver lining, although at times it's really hard to find it. I know I have to keep going as my little man is watching me, his mother, who's poorly with limitations, but a fighter who keeps on going.

'Superwoman', the Alicia Keys song, is played even more in my life now. Originally this song helped me when Luca died, although it's definitely one area of my life where the silver lining failed to appear. However, the words of Alicia Keys' song spoke out to me, as many of her songs do. My life did not seem complete. There was a big hole inside me, and my sorrow was weighing me down. But I knew I had to find the strength from somewhere.

I find that music and certain artists can play a big part in our lives. Lyrics and melodies can touch us in many ways and be very healing.

For example, when I split up with my first husband, Destiny's Child's song 'Survivor' was released. Lots of things were said to me by his family, but it was that 'Survivor' song that gave me the strength to stand up and say: "I'll show you. I am a survivor and will do better. I will have a good life; you have not taken that away from me" (paraphrasing the lyrics).

Summary

Whenever you think you're down for the count, and nothing is going to get you up, you have to know that there's always a way back. My fibromyalgia diagnosis totally knocked me for a loop and that same question was there again: "Why me?" While I was experiencing excruciating and debilitating pain it forced me to do a lot of soul-searching. I was being challenged again, but I knew I just had to deal with every day the best way I could. It's a matter of putting one foot in front of the other and knowing that there is light at the end of the tunnel. I constantly remind myself that I am an Angel Warrior! I am a Survivor! And it's this inner strength that pushes me forward to new beginnings.

I encourage you all to discover this inner strength. Be an Angel Warrior! Be a Survivor! Be a Superwoman! But, most of all be someone who thrives and who finds the silver lining in everything. It's always there.

Chapter Nine

Turning Point

So now I'll take you back to the time of my breakdown on Luca's 6th anniversary in June 2018, which actually became my breakthrough. What that did was make me the superwoman Alicia Keys' song talks about. It made me want to start a charity in Luca's memory. That charity would give a cuddle cot to all maternity units across the UK to ensure that bereaved parents in baby loss, don't go through what we did when we didn't have that cuddle cot. What is a cuddle cot, you may ask? A cuddle cot is a cooling mattress that's fitted into a chilled cot and helps preserve babies' bodies when they have passed. It slows down the deterioration of the baby's body, allowing the parents/family to have up to a week with their child to say goodbye.

Essentially, the cuddle cot gives the gift of time - precious time that parents will never have again with their newborn child. It's time for them to hold their baby and say goodbye before he or she is gone forever. Without a cuddle cot, parents would only have a few hours with their baby, as my husband and I did with our son, Luca. Unfortunately, cuddle cots had only recently become available, and the hospital didn't have any at that time.

This prompted me to launch a charity called The Luca Foundation, in November 2018. This was with the specific intent of raising funds to purchase cuddle cots for as many hospitals as possible. I never want another parent to have to suffer the sadness and terrible grief of having their baby taken away from them too soon.

With the help of fundraisers and supporters we raised over £8,500 in our first nine months. I was also nominated as an Inspirational Person of the Year for the Midlands Business and Community Charity Awards in November 2019, which was a huge and wonderful surprise for me. It meant that people recognised that I was using my sad experience and my grief to do something good for others, whilst suffering with the chronic illness of fibromyalgia.

During this time, there was some strange unknown tension building with someone well known to my family. None of us could actually put our finger on why it was there. Suddenly in November 2019, a huge argument erupted out of nowhere. After a few unkind words on a text, the person abruptly said, 'I want nothing to do with any of you, and you can keep fundraising for the dead baby!

It shocked the whole family that someone could even think such a thing, let alone type them into a text message. My brothers had to check that this person was in their right mind after realising what had been typed on this chat. The response was: 'Yes I mean it!' Since then, none of us has ever spoken to this person!

Apart from this, 2019 ended on a high for me. I'd accomplished so much with the charity and found my inner strength to manage my illness. It was still extremely hard at times and I was continuing to have very bad days. However, I would try not to let it get me down, I'd rest through those difficult times. I had also started writing this book ('Angel Warrior') as well as "Why Did Grandad Die"?

When 2020 arrived, I was full of hope and ambition, and excited about the year ahead. The Luca

Foundation became a registered charity on 6th January 2020, and it was a fantastic start to the year.

I named this book 'Angel Warrior' and I hope the name catches on and will be approved by bereaved parents. It would also be great if it could eventually be recognised as the name for a grieving parent.

At the same time, I wanted to create clothing, specifically tee-shirts, imprinted with the name 'Angel Warrior' not only to complement this book, but so that bereaved parents can honour the precious child they have lost by wearing an Angel Warrior tee-shirt or hoodie. Since I came up with this name and design for clothing, I've noticed that people who have not experienced the loss of a child are also attracted to the name. They may not have lost a child, but since most people have experienced death of a loved one in their lives, I would say that they are also angel warriors.

I then began to think of a few other mental health-oriented slogans I could put on clothing that would reflect a person's feelings.

I naturally did a lot of research before launching

my own clothing line, and sought guidance from Karen Heap at Orchard Business Development as well as the local Chamber of Commerce who provide free support for new business owners

I knew from the beginning that the clothing must be eco-friendly, not only helping the earth, but also animal friendly and devoid of toxins or chemicals. The company would then be called LK Eco Style. Since the slogans on the clothing are timeless and geared towards mental health, I intend for a percentage of profits from the sale of clothing to support charitable organisations eventually, such as the Samaritans, the NSPCC, war veterans, sports charities, the anti-knife crime charity, conservation and World Land Trust and of course The Luca Foundation.

As well as making sure that the clothing is suitable for all age groups, male and female, LK Eco Style will also eventually be supporting social campaigns and movements, including Black Lives Matter, Pride, and the Heads-Up campaign, which encourages men to speak out about mental health.

This was also a time for me to reclaim my independence. I had worked since I was sixteen but then having lost my career to fibromyalgia, I was now without an income. I was relying on my husband and I absolutely hated asking him for money. This book and my clothing line will give me an opportunity to be independent again. In addition, it's a way of helping others and of course paying tribute to Luca.

As you can imagine, my new venture has required a lot of thought and preparation, especially when I have had to work around my illness and my limitations. However, I have had the valuable support of Jas, my family and my friends, and am confident that the business will be a success...once we're back to 'normal'.

When the Coronavirus hit, I thought it would be difficult to start my projects, let alone finish them. Then Jas was furloughed from his job at a large car manufacturer in Coventry, which meant that I was able to apply for funding from the local council and charitable organisations to produce the children's book – "Why Did Grandad Die?". I also approached the Charities Commission asking for businesses to sponsor the book. So, in April I spent a lot of time filling in funding applications. Then by late May we had funds coming in to start phase one of the project: the illustrations.

In late May, my parents, who had seen me struggle for over three years, kindly gave me a loan so that I could start LK Eco Style and produce this 'Angel Warrior' book. They loved my business idea and knew it would be a great way for them to support me and help me regain control of my life. My mum was very pleased that I would also be supporting other charities through my business. I believe that if all businesses gave back just a little of their profits, the world would be a better place.

During my research I found that eco-friendly clothing was generally quite expensive to buy. Consequently, I looked long and hard for a good UK based supplier so that I could meet customer demand as the business grew. I knew from the outset that I would not be charging the exceedingly high prices that many other eco-friendly clothing companies charge. I ordered samples, and my family wore them, washed them, and checked for the durability of the fabric. It was also very important to me to ensure that child labour was not involved in the production; therefore, 'Fairtrade' was an absolute must! This means that all LK Eco Style clothing is made in humane conditions and the workers are paid fairly.

All my boxes were being ticked. Now I knew we could go ahead; so, for us, good was coming out of the lockdown. I was able to put all my time into my work with the added bonus of Jas being home to look after Ky. We shared the home-schooling and Jas did the grocery shopping once a week, suitably masked, naturally! It started to all come together with A LOT of resting in between too.

Mother's Day, our ten-year wedding anniversary and Ky's seventh birthday, were all celebrated during lockdown. We made the most of all the nice weather and counted our blessings that we had a garden and a portable pool we could all enjoy on the hot days. We participated in family quiz nights on Zoom, and I had regular girlie chats with my girlfriends on WhatsApp video calls too. What an unexpected blessing this great technology has been for us all. VE day celebrations were small, but we nonetheless marked this important date along with our neighbours and most of socially-distanced Great Britain! I checked in with my only remaining grandparent in Leicester every week, to make sure she was okay. Fortunately, my Uncle Pat lives near my grandma and did her shopping.

Things could have been a lot worse, but I was looking on the bright side as much as I could. I felt blessed for all the good in my life and began writing in a gratitude diary with Ky.

During this period of restriction, I was very much 'a girl on fire' (with a nod to another Alicia Keys' song). Along with launching my eco-friendly clothing line, LK Eco Style, in the summer of 2020, I had completed my children's book, "Why Did Grandad Die?", for The Luca Foundation, and this book ('Angel Warrior'), was almost completed.

Schools started back in September, with necessary protection in place to make sure our children were safe from the virus. My parents were able to go to Italy for a week, which was amazing for them, and we were thrilled to be taking care of their German Shepherd, 'Troy' while they were gone. Jas enjoyed taking him for walks and Ky loved playing fetch in the garden with the dog. In fact, we actually saw such a difference in Ky - he was so energised and excited being with Troy that we started to seriously consider getting a dog for him. We knew exactly what we wanted: a dog that didn't shed hair, a smaller breed because our home is not very big, and a dog that, as Ky said, “I can pick up and cuddle”. So, I began looking out for poodle, mix, cross or miniature at local rescue centres, but none were available.

In October 2020, I had a special mention at the ‘Woman Who, Solopreneur Awards’, for all my accomplishments, which was a lovely surprise.

Unfortunately, LK Eco Style wasn’t doing very well, so I redesigned some of the clothing, with the help of a dear friend, and my web designer. These were successful and brought in a few sales before Christmas.

In December, I was again surprised with the honour of becoming Take a Break magazine’s, ‘1 in 30 Amazing Women in the UK’, for their 30th anniversary year. My friend Amanda had nominated me, and out of thousands of entries I was one that they chose. It was such a thrill! I posted the article on social media and received so many congratulatory messages. It still excites me to this day!

With many wonderful things happening, a lockdown at Christmas was disappointing for all of us. We really missed being with the rest of my family, as well as all the fun, games, laughter and food. In comparison, the three of us had a very quiet Christmas - Ky was very happy with his Star Wars and Ninjago Lego sets and was extremely good at putting it all together. His concentration level was phenomenal, and both Jas and I thought that we might have a future engineer in our midst. However, Ky tells us that he wants to be a footballer, or maybe a golfer! Of course, in a few years he may even want to be a fireman! So many options ahead of him and it's going to be very exciting to see how my son develops over the years of his life.

I did feel the loss of Luca a lot more this Christmas, which made me realise how much I needed my family and friends during the festive season to stop reminding me of my loss. It never goes away!

In between Christmas and New Year, I found out that miniature poodle puppies had been born quite locally. We had a family meeting-and decided to buy one of these puppies. Ky was excited beyond belief that he was going to finally have a dog! We opted for the large white male pup in the litter, which ticked all our boxes. We decided he would be called 'Remy'. This was the name I had chosen for our third child that we sadly were unable to have, due to my illness.

New Year's Eve was the first time Ky stayed up with us to watch the fireworks and see the New Year in, and he loved it! Then just as we were ready to send him off to school, the third lockdown began, and it hit me hard, mentally. Jas was not furloughed, and I could not operate my business to earn a living, complete this 'Angel Warrior' book, run The Luca Foundation charity and home school, all at the same time!

I was finding it very difficult, and Jas didn't seem to understand what I was going through. We were having arguments, which led to Ky and myself going to my parents for a couple of nights for some respite. This turned into four nights as Ky didn't want to leave Troy, their dog. Once we were back home, things were so much better, and it was clear that having a few days apart had done us all good.

We hadn't taken delivery of the poodle puppy yet, but were sent regular photos, videos and did Facetime with Remy's breeder so that we could see him. One time he was feeding with the other puppies and kept being pushed away from one of his sisters. A few days later we got a video of him snapping back at his sister for biting at him. He was already keeping us entertained, which was lovely. Ky by now was counting down the days for us to collect Remy and marking it on the calendar. Only two weeks to go and he would be home with us on the first Saturday in February.

Jas took care of night training with Remy as I have to take a cocktail of medication to help my pain and to sleep at night. Ky and I did the daytime training and I gave him a little bit of pocket money for helping. It also gave him a chance to bond with Remy, which is great to see.

Final Summary

Between 2018 and early 2021, I learned a lot about myself. I found the strength to be the superwoman I needed to be, not just for myself, but for my young son, for my husband and for us as a family, whilst continuing to keep Luca's memory alive. I had to find a new way of living again as I was limited in what I could do both physically and mentally. When you're living with fibromyalgia, pretending to be someone that you're not and always saying: “I'm fine” when people ask how you are, is exhausting. I was not always fine, and many times I wanted to say that I was struggling big time. However, what was that person actually going to do to help me? Mentally, yes, it would have been better to get it off my chest and say that I wasn’t doing well, but quite honestly, I don’t think people wanted to hear that.

I often had nightmares during this period where I would be yelling at complete strangers who were looking at me bizarrely because of my limitations and my fragile mental state. In the nightmare I’m shouting at them, ‘I'm not well! I am not a well person!’ I think my subconscious was trying to tell me that I was locked into the body of someone I didn’t want to be. I wanted to scream and shout at people and say, “This is not me!” I believe a lot of my frustrations have been played out in my dreams. The frustrations I had about people not understanding fibromyalgia and judging me for my perceived weakness. More than anything, the frustration I had with myself in having to live with fibromyalgia. The other bad dreams I’ve had since the accident was having a car accident again. Over time since the accident, I have not liked driving in the dark, I would have nightmares of not being in control. Again, my subconscious playing out what that car accident has done to me, and it was out of my control. I would often mourn for my old life, when I was fit, active and able to anything.

It had stopped me from having a third child, it ended my career, it had changed our lives beyond recognition, and that was a hard blow to take. The only thing I could do now was really focus on my abilities, although I would get confused and mixed up with my words, due to the cognitive behavior of the fibro brain.

I also developed pain in my hands and my feet. So, whilst putting this book together, I was dictating it rather than typing it, because my hands hurt too much when I was writing on the computer. My feet would ache even when I was lying down, and I wasn't able to sleep, but Jas would manipulate my toes and massage my feet, and then I'd be able to sleep. I was experiencing quite a few restless nights, and a lot of my symptoms were getting worse. But I was determined to write this book, to help many of you out there who are Angel Warriors, as well as those who are supporting Angel Warriors, and now Fibro Warriors too, as I was focusing on my abilities and not my disabilities.

It's true that, without a doubt, every single person has experienced some kind of pain and loss in their lives, some at an early age. Everything that happens in life has an effect on us, for good or bad, and shapes us into the human beings we become. When I was eleven, my first cousin Sweetie, who was almost a year younger than me, was diagnosed with leukemia. I watched for a year as she battled the illness, helpless to do anything to make her feel better. At one stage she looked quite well, as if she was recovering, but a year later, she had deteriorated and sadly died. Sweetie was more than my first cousin, she was like a sister to me, and my best friend. She was the one I always hung out with in the school holidays, and we spent time together at every opportunity. I didn't like family get-togethers after that because Sweetie wasn't there, and I didn't really want to hang out with the rest of my younger cousins. I do think though that when we're younger we're more resilient, and I soon bounced back.

When I was fourteen-years old, I had to take the

bus to a school in Loughborough, a couple of towns away from where I lived. One day a lorry was overtaking on a blind bend and smashed into the side of the bus, sending it into a ditch. It was bad! Many of us were thrown from the bus and some of the children and the driver were admitted to intensive care. Fortunately, I wasn't hurt, apart from a flesh wound on my face, which didn't need stitches, only a bandage and I banged my head, but no concussion, thankfully. Again, I bounced back quite quickly.

At the age of sixteen I lost my first grandparent, my mum's father, my Papa. He had a heart attack on his way home from work. He was fifty-eight. It was hard to see my mum grieving so heavily, and even though I was working full time as a trainee bank cashier, I helped out as much as I could with my younger brothers, did the cooking and other chores.

When I was twenty-two, I entered into an arranged marriage with a man who, during our engagement period, pretended to be something he wasn't. I ended up with a husband who was physically, mentally and emotionally abusive, and I was so unhappy. I feel very grateful that with the support of my family, I was able to get out of the marriage. That was the best decision I've ever made, and I soon began to enjoy life again.

Luckily, with the help of my Christian faith, I've found strength within myself and have been able to survive hardships. I thought I'd be able to handle anything, but I was not prepared for the hardship of losing Luca. This was the one time I never thought I'd be able to survive, and when I thought of taking my own life. But, with the grace of God, that darkness and desire to end my life disappeared. Losing your child is absolutely one of the worst life experiences imaginable. It is a loss that changes a parent forever.

Eventually I found the strength to carry on and have our second son, return to work and start enjoying life again. I was disappointed that I was unable to conceive another child with my husband, Jas, especially as I considered myself fit and healthy. I was always very active.

Little did we know that all of this was about to change drastically. My life would never be the same again because a young girl chose to use her phone whilst driving her car.

My son, now eight years old, doesn't remember the days when I used to play football with him in the garden, take him to the park and have fun running around playing hide-and-seek. I'm afraid that Ky's childhood memories of me will only be that I was either sleeping or in too much pain to spend time with him. Hopefully over time, he'll remember that I tried my best to do as much as I could for him. My son is the reason that I'm able to move ahead with my creative ventures. He inspired me to write my children's book, "Why Did Grandad Die?" after the question he asked about Luca's death. He has also given me the strength to write 'Angel Warrior' and explain my journey as a bereaved parent.

I don't think I could cope with everything in my life since the illness, if I hadn't had Ky. I wouldn't want to be here without him. Previously it was Jas who saved my life, but people change after the loss of a child. We're not the same people we each married; and why would we be after everything that's happened? Most certainly the added stress and strain of my illness, as well as the extra responsibility Jas has had to deal with, has made it difficult for him.

The way we keep Luca alive is also different for

both of us. It seems that it's common for men and women to grieve in their own way, which can sometimes cause friction in a marriage. Jas is more internal with his feelings, whereas I'm vocal as I want to 'break the silence' and taboo of not talking about child loss or bereavement as a whole. It is one of the causes of mental health issues across the world, not just the UK. However, by being more vocal I have encouraged other mothers to contact me for support and inspired these women to open up about their baby loss. Of course, I'm not a trained counsellor, but have referred them on to other support charities. I had a wonderful message from a lady who I referred saying that I had changed her life, and that she was so grateful to me. It gives me such a wonderful feeling of satisfaction, knowing that I have helped other bereaved parents.

This is why this book is written from my perspective not my husband's.

Whilst Jas has been the sole supporter of our family for the last three and a half years, it is now time for me to contribute and regain a little independence. I've had to think long and hard about what I might do, considering the disabilities I live with. I am fully aware that my knee will never be fully recovered, and as the doctor has told me will also not stop it from giving way as it does quite often. However, I hope that regular nerve block treatments will keep me walking at least a few steps at a time.

However, if the treatments are unsuccessful then I know that I have a team of reliable people who have helped to establish my clothing line, LK Eco Style, and will be there to help. I'm determined to be able to do as much as I can by myself, although I realise there will be times when I'm struggling and stuck in bed with no energy to do anything as again happened quite a lot recently. Unfortunately, that's the reality of my life at present, but I refuse to be a victim. I'm a fighter. I'm a warrior. I'm an Angel Warrior!

The way I see it, when Ky grows up and understands what his mum has gone through, he'll understand that it's important to show strength and courage during the hard times in life.

I hope my son will always think of me as a fighter who is determined to overcome any difficulties I might be facing. There are times though when it's been too difficult and, at the last minute, I've had to cancel the day out we'd planned together because of my chronic illness. It breaks my heart to disappoint my son, but I hope he knows that I did the best I could.

At times I get angry about what I've lost in my life, but then when I'm sitting with Ky and we're writing in the gratitude journal, I realise how fortunate I am to have been blessed with so much good.

Apart from my precious child, I have a wonderfully kind and supportive husband, as well as loving family and friends who have been there for me all these hard years and whilst I build my clothing business, LK Eco Style. With this business, I intend to help other non-profit charities, as well as making it easier for people to express their feelings by putting words onto a tee-shirt instead.

In addition, The Luca Foundation will honour and memorialise my child, Luca, and support other bereaved parents and families whose babies were born in the most traumatic of circumstances, by ensuring that all maternity units across the UK have working cuddle cots. If over time, as a non-profit charity, we can do more, then we are ready for that, for example we now also repair and service existing cuddle cots.

So, I ask you, the reader, to help us at The Luca Foundation to support bereaved families so that they can spend precious time with their baby and make memories that we were deprived of, but to also 'break the silence', and make talking about loss a normal conversation for our future generations to come.

If you are a person who favours ethical, sustainable eco-friendly clothing, I ask you to support my clothing line, LK Eco Style by purchasing any item at: www.lkecostyle.com.

You can also purchase your Angel Warrior tee-shirt from LK Eco Style.

Thank you for reading my book, and I hope I have been able to help my fellow Angel Warriors and Fibro Warriors, and those who support them through their hard journey.

To purchase 'Why Did Grandad Die?' or donate/fundraise towards a cuddle cot, please go to: www.thelucafoundation.org.uk

To purchase your Angel Warrior tee-shirt and book, please go to www.lkecostyle.com

Our social media handles are also on the websites, and in the future, I will be making regular posts on those platforms detailing the progress of The Luca Foundation. In addition, I will be talking to other Angel Warriors on a video streaming link to be launched 2021/22 on YouTube by LK Media.

I am on a mission to 'break the silence' on the taboo of not being able to talk about loss of any type. This leads to mental health issues, which is also now one of the leading causes of death in the modern world. I hope you will help spread the message too!

Watch this space for more from me. God bless you all xx Sharon xx

Printed in Great Britain
by Amazon

24563636R00148